# TOGETHER WE EQUIP

Integrating Discipleship and Ministry Leadership
for Holistic Spiritual Formation

## JODY DEAN and HAL STEWART

WESTBOW
PRESS®
A DIVISION OF THOMAS NELSON
& ZONDERVAN

WestBow Press books may be ordered through booksellers or by contacting:

WestBow Press
A Division of Thomas Nelson & Zondervan
1663 Liberty Drive
Bloomington, IN 47403
www.westbowpress.com
1 (866) 928-1240

ISBN: 978-1-9736-1963-5 (sc)
ISBN: 978-1-9736-1964-2 (hc)
ISBN: 978-1-9736-1962-8 (e)

Library of Congress Control Number: 2018901764

Print information available on the last page.

WestBow Press rev. date: 02/21/2018

# CONNECTING THE DOTS

## Dr. Chuck Kelley

I have been studying Southern Baptist evangelism for most of my adult life. The history, the statistics, the stories of how SBC churches go about the task of sharing the gospel with the lost in their communities have been a continual focus of my attention for decades. With growing concern I watched the growth of the SBC turn into a statistical plateau, and with even more concern; watched the early indicators of decline appear and grow. The questions of why decline was beginning to happen and what could be done to reverse it were matters of burning concern to me. How could we return to the evangelistic fruitfulness of days past?

And then, Hurricane Katrina happened. As president of New Orleans Baptist Theological Seminary, I became completely immersed in helping our school and families through the aftermath of America's worst natural disaster. One consequence of this was a complete break from all of my thinking and research in SBC evangelism. For more than a year, my research stopped and my attention was given entirely to recovery, until the day an invitation arrived. The North American Mission Board was bringing the evangelism leaders of the SBC to New Orleans, and they asked me to talk with them about the state of evangelism in the Convention. I did not realize it at the time, but that invitation would lead to a turning point in my understanding of why effective evangelism happens.

I returned to my research with fresh eyes from my time away, and I soon noticed two things. First, the SBC was clearly in decline. We were past the "early indicators" stage, and the downward trend in baptisms and other areas was present and gathering momentum. The second thing I noticed for the first time was a critical connection between evangelism and discipleship in Southern Baptist church life. To this day my lack of notice of the essential nature of this connection surprises me. I can only say I was so focused on direct evangelism that I did not adequately understand all that made evangelism effective. Here is what became clear:

Southern Baptists have long been known for a passionate, aggressive approach to evangelism and missions. That passion was a driving force in the creation of the SBC, and today it remains the strongest glue that holds the Convention together. We view ourselves and are viewed by others as evangelists among the families of American churches. What has been rarely noticed or commented on by ourselves and others is an equally passionate approach to discipleship in Southern Baptist life for a great many years. A shared strategic vision for evangelism and a shared strategic vision for discipleship shaped the culture and worldview of SBC churches and drove growth and expansion in SBC life. What I have learned is that those two visions were interdependent. They needed each other to retain vitality.

As time passed, the shared strategic vision for discipleship began to fade first, followed later by declining evangelistic fruitfulness and a fading strategic vision for evangelism. We worked harder and harder on evangelistic methodologies, but with little effect. Why does discipleship matter so much for evangelism? Every strategy and approach to evangelism is based upon one common assumption: the life of a person with Christ is different than the life of a person without Christ. The Great Commission calls the church to make disciples, both baptizing and teaching them. If we are going to reach people for Christ, we must be prepared to help them follow Him daily and become more and more like Him. Connecting the dots of discipleship and evangelism without losing focus on either one is essential for fruitful ministry.

The purpose of this book is to help you with the crucial task of the ongoing discipleship and ministry leadership of believers. As you read it, I would encourage you to keep in mind that this is one of the biggest challenges faced by congregations today. If we do not grow disciples, and if we do not encourage and teach Christlikeness to our people, we cannot fulfill the Great Commission. I salute the writers of this volume for taking on this topic, and I join them in praying that you will find it to be a useful tool.

# CONTENTS

## CHAPTER 1

# SPIRITUAL FORMATION

## Hal Stewart

> A good person produces good out of the good stored up in his heart. An evil person produces evil out of the evil store up in his heart, for his mouth speaks from the overflow of the heart. - Jesus Christ of Nazareth (Luke 6:45 CSB)[1]

Several years ago, I was able to give my wife Julie a strand of pearls and some pearl earrings that I bought while on a mission trip to Southeast Asia. At the time, I was intrigued by pearls, as many of the ones sold were not, in fact, real pearls. They were fake pearls that just looked like real pearls on the outside. I certainly did not want to give my wife some fake jewelry! So, I asked my friend and missionary, Ron, how a pearl is formed, in order to validate my purchase. Ron, a former high school science teacher, knew the process well. Ron explained that a spectacular pearl begins as a tiny piece of a seashell or a grain of sand. It could even begin as a parasite living in the oyster or mollusk. When it enters into the oyster's shell, irritation of its soft tissue slowly begins. Over time, the irritant then develops layers of nacre. The nacre builds up and strengthens the pearl, and it becomes larger and stronger. Ultimately, over a period of months and years, a beautiful shiny pearl develops. There are some similarities in the development of the pearl which can be compared to the process of spiritual formation in each human heart.

Scripture teaches that every person starts out as an irritant, being born with a sin nature. We are declared as enemies of God, being dead in our trespasses and sins (Eph. 2:1-4; Rom. 5:8-10). But, by God's amazing life-giving grace, those of us who believe in Christ are declared righteous before God. Slowly, but surely, God then envelops us in Himself and transforms us into beautiful followers who reflect His beauty.[2]

## CHRISTIAN FORMATION

Have you ever considered the fact that all people experience spiritual formation? All humans are created as holistic spiritual beings, influenced by both the nature of their personhood and the nurture of life experiences and environment. So, the depth and breadth of their spiritual formation are determined by a multitude of dynamics, beginning at birth and extending into adulthood. Over the last century, the philosophical paradigm shift from modernity to post-modernism has moved the needle from truth and rationalism to subjectivity and relativism. Though we are shaped by culture, social systems, beliefs, and institutions, that type of formation is not exactly the same thing as being shaped by Jesus. Simply put, it is not a spiritual formation in the sense in which we speak of Christ being formed in you. So for the purposes of this chapter, I am referring to spiritual formation meaning Christian formation.

Understanding spiritual formation is vital for discipleship leaders and ministry leadership. Recently, George Barna has stated, "Christianity would be incredibly influential in our culture if Christians consistently lived their faith. The problem is that millions do not live like Christians, partly because they don't know how."[3] God created all men with the capacity to become "formed" spiritually. How that spiritual formation occurs is the central theme of this chapter. This chapter focuses on Christian spiritual formation, which is centered on Christlikeness as both the means and product of the formation. Dallas Willard's definition explains spiritual formation as, "the process whereby the inmost being of the individual (the heart, will or spirit) takes on the quality or character of Jesus himself."[4]

Here is the wonderful news: by responding to God's grace and love found in Jesus Christ, we can be conformed to Christ's image through the work of the Holy Spirit. Romans 8:29 (CSB) indicates God's plan for those who begin the Christian spiritual formation process, "For those he foreknew he also predestined to be conformed to the image of his Son so that he would be the firstborn among many brothers and sisters." The very fact that Christian formation is achievable gives us hope to take steps forward, as we often struggle, fail and grow. It is a worthy goal to understand formation in a way whereby we can apply some newfound understandings to practical ministry in local churches.

## THE UNIFYING PRINCIPLE

What drives and motivates you in life? Where does your satisfaction come from? Most people answer these questions with temporary rather than eternal values. Yet the underlying answer to these questions reveals the fuel behind the spiritual formation process. The biblical aim in life is simply the glory of God (1 Cor. 10:31). And therefore, the aim of formation is the glory of God. In other words, the key principle for our lives should be the magnification of God's glory every moment we live. John Piper summed this principle up by stating, "God is most glorified in us when we are most satisfied in Him."[5] Therefore, the advancement of God's kingdom, His reign, and rule on earth, happens through us, His bride, the church. Although the spiritual formation process is about God's glory, it ultimately leads to others coming into fellowship with God. The apostle John shared this in John 15:8 (CSB) "My Father is glorified by this: that you produce much fruit and prove to be my disciples." God the Father is glorified when disciples make disciples. The spiritual formation process is for God, yet results in our lives impacting others.

Being formed into the identity of Christ is the standard; or baseline, for us. But, how does this formation resulting in spiritual maturity actually happen? I intend to explain the process by suggesting principles, and then to identify the useful application for discipleship and ministry leadership. Thus, the purpose of this chapter is two-fold. I aim to explain the basic tenets of God's pathway to spiritual maturity and subsequently to offer suggestions on how churches can integrate these tenets into ministry methods and programming.

## SPIRITUAL FORMATION PRINCIPLES

The following story is an analogy to help you better understand spiritual formation. Learning to ride a bike is a common experience for most people. Maybe you remember learning to ride a bike as a child. I distinctly remember my experience learning to ride as a six-year-old. All too often, I fell off the bike and injured, scuffed up, cut, and bruised my knees or elbows. I did learn to ride with help from my dad. He would hold the bike for me and walk along beside me as I learned to balance and pedal the bike. After time and lots of practice, I rode by myself and traveled faster through the yard and driveway of our home, and around obstacles like trees. But, I did not become a skilled or competent bike rider overnight. It took time. I learned that when I pushed the pedal of the bike with my right foot, the left pedal did not remain static. It moved around with the force of the right pedal. The faster I pedaled, the faster the opposite pedal turned. I also needed help from my dad, who was more mature than me. I had to fall down and learn many times. But, I was committed to learning how to ride.

Here are the spiritual formation principles that can be seen from this personal illustration: spiritual formation takes time and commitment, just as learning to ride a bike does. Just as we pushed the pedal to ride the bike, we must learn to obey God's Word. This requires the personal volitional choice to obey God. When we obey

God, his mighty power and the work of the Holy Spirit will grow us as believers. As we walk through life, we may fall down as we learn certain truths, as we are corrected by more mature believers, and as we experience hardships. With God's grace, we get back up and keep persevering through life's journeys. Sometimes, we learn the greatest truths about God and his wonderful grace when we fall on hard times. We also need a spiritual parent to come along beside us to help us grow. Spiritual formation is most effective in the context of relationships.

God's word provides for us the blueprint for spiritual formation. Even a scant survey of the sacred Scriptures provides meaningful insight for regarding spiritual formation. Therefore, the foundational explanation for spiritual formation is dependent upon reading and studying the truths found in God's word. Let us briefly examine four formation principles that the Apostle Paul wrote about to the early believers ("little Christs") who would form spiritually in a manner worthy of Christ. The following spiritual formation principles provide direction for personal and corporate application to be more Christ-like:

*New Creation*

Paul reminded us, "My children, I am again suffering labor pains for you until Christ is formed in you" (Galatians 4:19 CSB). The key word is *formation*, from the root word *morphe*.[6] This word is translated *transformed* in 2 Corinthians 3:18 CSB, "We all, with unveiled faces, are looking as in a mirror at the glory of the Lord and are being transformed into the same image from glory to glory; this is from the Lord who is the Spirit." This means that the inner person is changed, or transformed, by becoming completely different. God remakes a person into a "new creation." The formation process begins by receiving Christ as Savior and Lord, subsequently valuing him above all, and organizing personal behaviors around the new desires and will. This process occurs incrementally and comes from God's Spirit. Knowledge of God and truth alone is not enough; rather, the transformation includes the reshaping and remolding of our spirit to align with Christ.

## Inside Out Change

Here is a powerful passage from the Apostle Paul: "Do not be conformed to this age, but be transformed by the renewing of your mind, so that you may discern what is the good, pleasing, and perfect will of God. (Romans 12:2 CSB). This indicates an inner transformation that begins with the mind and heart. The world's process of transformation is always opposite, as it is from the outside in. The world always measures by behavior, the looks, and the performance. But God changes the heart through the transformation of the mind. A.W. Tozer reminds us that the mind matters because "The most important thing about a man is what comes into his mind when he thinks of God."[7] Yes, we have to choose what we fill our minds with on a daily basis. Dallas Willard reminds us, "The process of spiritual formation in Christ is one of progressively replacing destructive images and ideas with images and ideas that fill the mind of Jesus himself."[8] Jesus clearly explained this principle, "And he said, "What comes out of a person is what defiles him. For from within, out of people's hearts, come evil thoughts, sexual immoralities, thefts, murders, adulteries, greed, evil actions, deceit, self-indulgence, envy, slander, pride, and foolishness. All these evil things come from within and defile a person.'" (Mark 7:20-23 CSB). Jesus addressed the core of the issue. The "Jesus" transformation happens from within.

## Personal Devotion

Paul wrote to the Ephesian church, "until we all reach unity in the faith and in the knowledge of God's Son, growing into maturity with a stature measured by Christ's fullness (Ephesians 4:13 CSB). The word "knowledge" is *epignosis*, which refers to experiential knowledge.[9] This means that maturity grows when we are involved, actively participating in the known object, which is God. Spiritual formation is not a passive process. One has to choose to learn and follow God and serve actively in the ministries of His bride, the church. Maturity in this text indicates a balance between theological knowledge and devotional intimate knowledge. Knowledge of spiritual formation cannot be without devotion to God.

## Relationships

In God's very nature, a relational dimension exists in the Trinity. God the Father, the Son Jesus, and the Holy Spirit relate interdependently to each other. Theologian Stanley Grenz offers, "God is best viewed as a social Trinity."[10] The Godhead is our model. Our quest for Christlikeness necessitates an integral community of relationships. Relationships begin in the family of origin and are further developed and united spiritually in the body of Christ. God's servant Paul pointedly expressed God's design for family and church relationships, "We proclaim him, warning and teaching everyone with all wisdom, so that we may present everyone mature in Christ" (Colossians 1:28 CSB). The end goal is to communicate the Gospel message to others for edification and spiritual growth. The spiritual formation process then aids each person to become spiritually mature. Diane Chandler concludes that "God has hardwired us to walk through life together in family relationships and in the body of Christ, the church, in order to fashion us increasingly into the image of God through the relational formation."[11]

## OUR GREATEST NEED

Human needs exist in the lives of people and have an effect on the spiritual formation process. At the most basic level of needs, we all need a relationship with Jesus Christ (Rom 3:23, 5:8). Yet some specific needs are different within all the various adult groupings—children, youth, singles, young marrieds, and seniors—because of differing human development tasks and learning. In similar seasons of life, such as family, marriage, retirement, and career, the needs are more general. Specific or real needs refer to an individual's personal experiences, such as a failing marriage, tragedies, present difficulties, and struggles. Recognizing the need to grow into Christlikeness due to the specific or real need of is part of the spiritual formation process.

When the greatest need is fulfilled by regeneration in an individual's life, the position before God is completely perfect. This is the beginning of spiritual formation and the product as well! While God sees the person as righteous, the individual still needs to develop and grow in holiness. Part of this process is becoming more and more satisfied in Christ as we grow. Christian educators Rick and Shera Melick explain, "We live in a developmental sphere of life where progressive changes make us what we need to be. While we are complete in what God has done for us, providing everything at the cross, we are incomplete as we live on earth."[12] The process of growing and transforming to a fully developed follower of Christ comes incrementally and is largely affected by the needs we have. Ultimately, our greatest need in salvation involves a positional, progressive, perfective aspect:

- _Positional Sanctification_. When you believed in Christ as your Savior, you were once-for-all, instantaneously set apart for God (Heb 10:10). This aspect is also called _justification_.
- _Progressive Sanctification_. This aspect refers to your daily growth in holiness (2 Cor 7:1). This is the outworking of practical disciplines of obedience and the Holy Spirit working.
- _Perfective Sanctification_. This aspect takes place when you see Christ as he is and become eternally like Him (1 John 3:2). This aspect is also called _glorification_.[13]

These aspects help to explain the means and end to spiritual formation leading to eternal life. The beginning point to Christian spiritual formation is observing and accepting the life of the perfect man, Jesus. The ending point, until we enter into eternity, is to live like Christ, or more precisely to abide in Christ. John described this goal in 1 John 2:6 (CSB), "The one who says he remains in him should walk just as he walked." Thus, the best way to grow in Christlikeness is to examine the spiritual disciplines that Jesus observed when he lived on earth.

## SPIRITUAL DISCIPLINES

In my life, I desire to be like Christ and make decisions that honor him. Yet, I too often regret some of my thoughts, attitudes, and actions. Therefore, it is important to understand that the spiritual formation process is simply becoming more spiritually mature. In his profound book *The Practice of the Presence of God,* Brother Lawrence wrote of being so in tune to God's presence that he was acutely aware of what would please and honor God, and he would then carry out those godly desires. Likewise, I must learn to practice being more aware of God's presence, which is best accomplished through spiritual disciplines.

If we were to consider all the thoughts, attitudes, words, and actions that we make in a day, would they reflect Christ, and be in tune with God? Each day is a training day. Just as an athlete trains for a game, so do spiritual disciplines help to train us in Christlikeness. Paul wrote, "And whatever you do, in word or in deed, do everything in the name of the Lord Jesus, giving thanks to God the Father through him." (Colossians 3:17 CSB). A great working definition of spiritual disciplines are those practices that help us to abide in God's presence.

It is helpful to explain what the spiritual disciplines are not. First, spiritual disciplines are not a means to maturity in and of themselves. They are not a barometer of my spirituality. Indeed, they are God-pleasing habits or practices for the believer, but the purpose is to provide a way for believers to grow into mature disciples of Jesus. Second, the disciplines are not a method to earn favor with God to make him love us any more than he already does.[14] God's love for us was settled on the cross.

A study of the Bible does not contain a list of such activities in a particular passage, but some authors have organized the spiritual practices to help us understand them more fully. Dallas Willard in his book *Spirit of the Disciplines* categorized these practices into disciplines of abstinence and disciplines of engagement. In his book *Celebration of Discipline,* Richard Foster has labeled these disciplines as inward disciplines, outward disciplines, and corporate disciplines. Most recently, David Mathis, in his book *Habits of Grace*, organized the disciplines into habits of the Word, habits of prayer, and habits of fellowship. He adds disciple-making and stewardship of possessions and time in a separate category.

As is evident, the precise number of spiritual disciplines varies from writer to writer. The important principle to remember is the purpose for practicing spiritual discipline which is to be more spiritually mature and more Christlike. Repetition helps us to practice being in God's presence. Undoubtedly, there are some disciplines that prove to be quite purposeful and effective by their very nature. While the human effort aspect of spiritual disciplines is vital, let us remember that God is working in our lives. Acknowledging the unparalleled work of God in individual's lives, Pazmino states, "There is no teacher like God the Father, Son, and Spirit. They have taught humanity since time began."[15] Pazmino explains the divine effort of God in the spiritual formation process, "Persons can be activated by the Holy Spirit who is present in human life to realize this potential of transformation in Christ personally and corporately. The Holy Spirit encounters the human spirit and makes transformation possible across the lifespan."[16]

## PRACTICAL INSIGHTS AND SUGGESTIONS

Almost every church ministry leader that I know yearns for church members who are growing, maturing, and living for Christ Jesus. When I served as a discipleship pastor, I was praying, seeking, and searching for the "Christlikeness church member" all the time. In fact, I would carry around a little red notebook in my pocket, and when I met people, I would write names down and follow-up with them to evaluate their spiritual maturity to help plug them into a ministry setting.

Not only is this a worthy desire of church ministry leaders, but, more importantly, it is God's plan and will for our lives. Paul wrote in 2 Corinthians 3:18 (CSB), "We all, with unveiled faces, are looking as in a mirror at the glory of the Lord and are being transformed into the same image from glory to glory; this is from the Lord who is the Spirit." This verse indicates that the spiritual formation process is progressive, and initiated by God. What, then, is our role individually, and corporately as a body in the spiritual formation process? The following are some principles that need to be applied personally and corporately in church ministry programming. Let us remember the pearls for a moment. There are some significant points of application that we should be reminded of and put into practice:

- *Salvation is needed.* The spiritual formation process is for everyone. We cannot assume that everyone who attends church is a believer. But, everyone is born with the need of salvation. In the beginning of the pearl making process, the pearls are simply broken shells or sand or just parasite food. Likewise, we are dead, useless in our transgressions, and then we are made alive in Christ. Therefore, the unifying principle of spiritual formation is to reach the world for Christ. Church Programs and ministry plans need to always be outward oriented, rather than focusing on inward needs.

- *Spiritual Formation is a process.* As explained, it takes a long time, sometimes several years, for a pearl to develop into a beautiful jewel. Likewise, we as believers go through trials, desert times, and often we are in the thorns by our own choosing. Every time we go through a trial, it is as if we are getting another layer of "mother of pearl" – layer upon layer, trial upon trials so that we are set apart for God's exclusive use with spiritual maturity in mind. John R. Tyson explains the timing of the process, "There are few shortcuts in the journey from being a sin-dominated person to becoming a spiritually empowered, Christ-like person; it is not a journey made quickly or easily."[17] This reminds us to never give up on people. It also reminds us to realize that all people are in the process, and sometimes more grace is needed when people struggle with commitments or disappoint us with lifestyles choices.

- *Obedience rules the day.* - Every oyster has the potential to develop a pearl. Every oyster or mollusk can produce a pearl, but some do not, or some never reach a useable size. Likewise, if we choose to let God empower us, he will do it. So we can become useful for His service and grow to great depths of spiritual maturity. Our heavenly Father's desire is clear: "If you are ridiculed for the name of Christ, you are blessed, because the Spirit of glory and of God rests on you. Let none of you suffer as a murderer, a thief, an evildoer, or a meddler" (1 Peter 1:14-15 CSB). Obedience to God leads to holiness and the life he offers. Here's the application. We need to take God's word seriously. Sin offends a Holy God and stifles our walk with him. Ministry leaders should have high expectations for their volunteers and always speak truth into their lives. Holiness is a high calling.

- *Every person is unique.* Natural pearls are different sizes and colors, and none are exactly alike. We also are all different and unique and just like the apostles, we have different gifts and abilities and are in different stages of spiritual growth. Simply put, DNA is different. Most of us have been given unique experiences for use in God's church. The beauty of the body of Christ is the diversity of the body. We have different functions, passions, experiences, and responsibilities that accentuate church unity for the "greater good."

Questions for Reflection:

1. How has your family of origin influenced your Christian spiritual formation? Has culture, social systems, beliefs, and institutions shaped your Christian spiritual formation in a positive way? Read Colossians 2:7-8.

2. What drives and motivates you in life? Where does your satisfaction come from? Read Ecclesiastes 3:10-11.

3. Dallas Willard reminds us, "The process of spiritual formation in Christ is one of progressively replacing destructive images and ideas with images and ideas that fill the mind of Jesus himself." Identify thought patterns and habits of your mind that are antithesis to the mind of Jesus. Read 2 Corinthians 10:5-6.

4. List as many spiritual disciplines of abstinence and engagement and as you can. Consider reviewing Richard Foster's book, *Celebration of Discipline* and Donald Whitney's *Spiritual Disciplines of the Christian Life*. List strong and weak disciplines in your spiritual growth process.

5. Your Christian spiritual formation is a journey. Consider the past week, month, and year. Write down some watermark moments where you experienced viable spiritual growth. For each moment, thank God and ask him to continue to help you grow. Read Philippians 1:6; 2:12-13.

## CHAPTER 2

# CULTURAL ENGAGEMENT

## Scott Jones

*Exegeting the culture has never been more important. Christianity in the West has been marginalized by the prevailing winds of Secularism, driven by the engine of globalization that will continue to exert significant pressure on the ministry of the Church in various contexts. . . . This is our journey, to engage culture through the Gospel as a missionary people.*[18]

During the early part of summer 2017, my wife and I celebrated our 25th wedding anniversary by taking a trip to several Caribbean islands. One of the islands we visited was Saint Martin or Sint Maarten; what one calls this island depends upon which part of the island you are referencing. The northern part of the island is Saint Martin and is an overseas collectivity of France; the southern part of the island is Sint Maarten and is a constituent country of the Kingdom of the Netherlands. As we planned our visit, we talked with a tour specialist about various excursions we could take. He emphatically stated to us that it all depended upon what type of cultural experience we wanted to have. Because of the distinct cultures of the Netherlands and France, our experience was contingent upon which part of the island we chose to visit. Ultimately, we decided to visit the southern part of the island;

and we had a fantastic time experiencing the Dutch culture of Sint Maarten.

## DEFINING TERMS

Culture has a significant influence not only upon vacation experiences but also upon every aspect of life. How one engages with culture is a significant factor in relation to Christian discipleship and ministry leadership. In order to realize this impact, it is best to first define certain key terms. First, and obviously, having a good working definition of *culture* is of paramount importance. Paul Hiebert defined culture as, "the more or less integrated system of ideas, feelings, and values and their associated patterns or behavior and products shared by a group of people who organize and regulate what they think, feel, and do."[19] Geert Hofstede further defined culture as, "the collective programming of the mind that distinguishes the members of one group from another. It is the software behind how we operate."[20]

As seen from these definitions, culture is a much more complex idea than simply the visible, outer aspects of culture. Furthermore, culture is primarily corporate, rather than individualistic, in nature. When addressing the relationship between exegeting culture and the missional nature of the church, Stetzer emphasized the importance for ministry leaders to identify *tribes*. Seth Godin defined a tribe as, "a group of people connected to one another, connected to a leader, and connected to an idea. . . .A group needs only two things to be a tribe: a shared interest and a way to communicate."[21]

In order to be most effective with discipleship and ministry leadership, the ministry leader must have a thorough understanding of the cultural tribes he engages. This reality leads to the next key term that must be defined: *understanding*. Duane Elmer defined understanding as, "the ability to see patterns of behavior and values that reveal the integrity of a people. Let me say it another way: understanding another culture is the ability to see how the pieces of the cultural puzzle fit together and make sense to them and you."[22]

By having an accurate understanding of the culture of the people to whom one is ministering, the ministry leader can be more effective in seeing things from their perspective. Thus, the next key term that needs to be defined is *perspectivism*. Elmer described perspectivism as, "you begin to see as the local people see. It's like having double vision: seeing the world through your own cultural lenses and also being able to see more and more clearly through the lenses of another culture."[23] Why is perspectivism so important for the ministry leader in relation to discipleship and ministry leadership? Because having such perspective allows the ministry leader to contextualize his efforts for maximum effectiveness. Therefore, *contextualization*, and not relevancy, is the ultimate goal for cultural exegesis. Contextualization has been aptly defined as, "taking the gospel to a new context and finding appropriate ways to communicate it so that it is understandable to the people in that context. Contextualization refers to more than just theology; it also includes developing church life and ministry that is biblically faithful and culturally appropriate."[24] As seen from the opening quote in this chapter, the need for the ministry leader to exegete culture has never been more necessary for participation in God's kingdom mission.

## THE NEED FOR CULTURAL INTELLIGENCE

David A. Livermore comprehensively describes the idea of a cultural intelligence quotient (CQ) which, "measures the ability to effectively reach across the chasm of cultural differences in ways that are loving and respectful."[25] In this quotient, cultural intelligence is composed of four factors: knowledge CQ, interpretive CQ, perseverance CQ, and behavioral CQ. The one central motivating factor, however, is love. Without love as the primary motive, the ministry leader will not have a high cultural intelligence quotient and thus will not be as effective in discipleship and ministry leadership.

*Factors*

Even with love, however, these other factors are necessary to be culturally intelligent in ministry. First, the ministry leader must possess a knowledge CQ; this quotient relates to "one's understanding of cross-cultural issues and differences." In relation to this necessary understanding, Elmer portrays culture using the image of an iceberg. In this image, he divides culture into two components: cultural artifacts and cultural values and assumptions. Cultural artifacts are pictured as the part of the iceberg that is above the surface of the water and includes "art, clothing, food, money, customs, gestures." Cultural values and assumptions are pictured as the part of the iceberg that is below the surface of the water and includes "unconscious, taken for granted beliefs, perceptions, and feelings."[26]

The next factor of cultural intelligence quotient is interpretive CQ. This factor refers to "the degree to which we're mindful and aware when we interact cross-culturally." Primarily, this part of cultural intelligence is related to discovering cultural preferences. Interpretive CQ, in relation to cultural exegesis, has to do with the ability to discern whether cultural preferences are good or right, bad or wrong, or in the middle or different.[27] Perseverance CQ is the next factor of the cultural intelligence quotient. This factor refers to "our level of interest, drive, and motivation to adapt cross-culturally." When we engage in perseverance CQ, many times people's behaviors that are part of a cultural pattern which seems foolish or illogical at first glance begin to make rational sense as we consider the foundational reasons.[28] The final factor of the cultural intelligence quotient is behavioral CQ. This factor refers to "the extent to which we *appropriately* change our verbal and nonverbal actions when we interact cross-culturally." When considering appropriate culture behavior, there are several sets of cultural values that must be discerned: identity orientation – individualism versus collectivism; hierarchy – top-down versus flat; risk – tight versus loose; time – polychromic versus monochromic; communication – explicit versus explicit; and achievement – being versus doing.[29]

Another critical factor of cultural intelligence in relation to discipleship and ministry leadership, which is primarily, but not only, linked to knowledge CQ, is the need for the ministry leader to properly exegete self. This has to do with examining ourselves and our ministry. Several helpful tips for proper self-exegesis include:

1.  Exegete yourself first before you exegete the culture.

2.  Exegete the culture of your particular church or ministry.

3.  Fall in love with the people and the place where God has placed you.

4.  Do not love and hold on to certain ideals, and thus build a church culture, that does not reflect the church around you in the ways it appropriately should.[30]

## EXEGETING THE CULTURE

*Biblical Foundation*

The need to exegete the culture for ministry is not new and particular to this period of history. Actually, cultural exegesis has been a part of the New Testament church from its beginning. One only has to look in the book of Acts to see this reality. Throughout Acts, one can readily see the continual crossing of boundaries and the transformation of cultures as part of the early church narrative. As Jesus commanded his apostles in Acts 1:8, we see the fulfillment of that command as the gospel moved and transformed cultures beginning in Jerusalem and moving to the ends of the earth. Ever since those days, various cultures have been properly exegeted by church leaders in such a manner that disciples have been made and church leaders have been developed. One central church leader in the New Testament who was adept at cultural exegesis was the apostle Paul. Stetzer wrote that "The

Acts 17 narrative of Paul's Gospel encounter in Athens offers a good model for us today. Our efforts in mission must always be sensitive to the life situations of the different groups of people we encounter."[31] Ministry leaders today can learn much about how to properly exegete the culture from Paul's example.

### Statistics

One helpful way to properly exegete the culture is through the appropriate use of statistics. Ministry leaders should never change personal or corporate beliefs based upon statistics; however, they "can be used in the following ways: to help define reality, to teach people and to help leaders make strategic decisions."[32] However, instead of seeing statistics as an ally, some ministry leaders see statistics as an enemy to the mission. It is imperative that ministry leaders appropriately exegete the culture, and the use of statistics is one significant way to help with that. Why is this the case? Because as previously mentioned, the need for cultural exegesis has never been more important. Erich Baumgartner argued, "More and more evidence points to the fact that the culture-inspired invisible assumptions, values, and norms that leaders bring with them create a distance between leaders working next door to each other that may be harder to bridge than the distance to a team member across continents."[33]

### Guiding Principles

As ministry leaders engage the contemporary culture in discipleship and ministry leadership, it is imperative that these leaders have a high cultural intelligence quotient about how individuals of that culture view themselves, the Christian faith, and the Christian church. An accurate assessment of the Western culture can be seen in the words of David Kinnaman and Gabe Lyons who said, "As Christianity has been ushered out of our social structures and off the cultural main stage, it has left a vacuum in its place. And the broader culture is trying to fill the void."[34] Kinnaman and Lyons further argue that the new moral code of America can be summed up in six guiding principles. The following principles are the percentages of people who completely agree or somewhat agree based on their survey:

Table 1: The percentages of people who completely agree or somewhat agree based on Kinnaman and Lyons survey.

| Guiding Principles | All US Adults | Practicing Christians |
|---|---|---|
| *To find yourself, look within yourself.* | 91% | 76% |
| *People should not criticize someone else's life choices.* | 89% | 76% |
| *To be fulfilled in life, pursue the things you desire most.* | 86% | 72% |
| *Enjoying yourself is the highest goal in life.* | 84% | 67% |
| *People can believe whatever they want as long as those beliefs do not affect society.* | 79% | 61% |
| *Any kind of sexual expression between two consenting adults is fine.* | 69% | 40% |

Related to this new moral code, the following statistics help paint a more specific picture of this cultural perspective of morality:

Table 2: Cultural Perspective of Morality.

| | Elders | Boomers | Gen-Xers | Millennials | Practicing Christians | No Faith | Other Faith |
|---|---|---|---|---|---|---|---|
| **1. Whatever is right for your life or works best for you is the only truth you can know.** | | | | | | | |
| Agree Strongly | 10% | 16% | 16% | 31% | 21% | 22% | 15% |
| Agree Somewhat | 29% | 31% | 43% | 43% | 20% | 45% | 41% |

| 2. Every culture must determine what is an acceptable morality for its people. | | | | | | | |
|---|---|---|---|---|---|---|---|
| Agree Strongly | 16% | 14% | 16% | 25% | 17% | 17% | 18% |
| Agree Somewhat | 44% | 46% | 51% | 45% | 30% | 51% | 42% |
| 3. The Bible provides us with moral truths that are the same for all people in all situations, without exception. | | | | | | | |
| Agree Strongly | 22% | 35% | 30% | 27% | 56% | 5% | 28% |
| Agree Somewhat | 37% | 27% | 29% | 29% | 27% | 22% | 25% |
| 4. Moral truth: absolute or relative? | | | | | | | |
| Absolute | 33% | 42% | 33% | 31% | 59% | 15% | 38% |
| Relative | 39% | 41% | 44% | 51% | 28% | 61% | 43% |
| Never thought about it | 28% | 17% | 23% | 19% | 14% | 23% | 19%[35] |

Focusing more closely upon one of the above-mentioned generations, Millennials, the following statistics give a portrait of wide-held cultural values and assumptions of this particular generation concerning Christianity in general and the local church in particular. When a sample of Millennial Christian churchgoers and outsiders were presented with the question "Here are some words or phrases that people could use to describe a religious faith. Please indicate if you think each of these phrases describes present-day Christianity", their responses were as follows:

Table 3: Descriptions of Present-Day Christianity

| Descriptions | Churchgoers | Outsiders |
|---|---|---|
| Anti-homosexual | 80% | 91% |
| Judgmental | 52% | 87% |
| Hypocritical | 47% | 85% |
| Old-fashioned | 36% | 78% |
| Too involved in politics | 50% | 75% |
| Out of touch with reality | 32% | 72% |
| Insensitive to others | 29% | 70% |
| Boring | 27% | 68% |
| Not accepting of other faiths | 39% | 64% |
| Confusing | 44% | 61% |

When another sample of Millennials who had left the church was asked why they had left the church, the reasons they gave could be categorized into six broad reasons: the church is overprotective, shallow, repressive, anti-science, exclusive, and doubtless.[36] These statistics, among other present cultural realities, must cause the ministry leader to ask the important question, "How can people of faith contribute to a world that, more and more, believes religion is bad?"[37] Particularly, in light of the topic of this chapter, the question must be asked, "How can the ministry leader engage effectively in discipleship and ministry leadership in the midst of this overwhelming cultural perspective?" This question is one the ministry leader cannot ignore and must give significant attention and effort to answering in a way that demonstrates cultural intelligence and faithfulness to the authority of God's Word.

## FROM CULTURAL EXEGESIS TO CULTURAL ENGAGEMENT

A significant part of what discipleship entails and what ministry leadership is focused upon is related to how Christians can effectively engage their culture and the pressing social issues of that culture. In other words, the church has been called through the life-changing power of the gospel to a lifestyle that is counterculture. David Platt stated, "The gospel is the lifeblood of Christianity, and it provides the foundation for *countering culture*. For when we truly believe the gospel, we begin to realize that the gospel not only *compels* Christians to confront social issues in the culture around us. The gospel actually *creates a* confrontation with the culture around – and within – us."[38] The primary way the church can best function as counterculture is through effective discipleship. Kinnaman and Lyons asserted, "The church sets itself apart as a counterculture by devoting sustained energy to both inward and outward expressions of discipleship."[39] Platt argued that this outward expression of discipleship is best seen in the ways individual Christians, families, and churches live out a "more consistent, Christ-compelled, countercultural response to the most pressing social issues of our day", such as poverty, abortion, the number of orphans and widows, sex slavery, marriage, sexual morality, ethnicity, helping refugees, and religious liberty.[40]

Effective and contextualized engagement with the surrounding culture and related social issues is the result of a well-developed discipleship strategy and intentional ministry leadership. Such cultural engagement will not happen by chance, therefore the ministry leader must give significant focus on how to develop 'good faith' Christians who can live as salt and light in their particular culture. Kinnaman and Lyons proposed a simple yet effective framework for how ministry leaders can develop such 'good faith' Christians – ones that respond to current and future social issues in a culturally intelligent and biblically faithful manner:

Table 4: Reasons Standing in the of Involvement

| Reasons | Practicing Christians | Non-Practicing Christians |
|---|---|---|
| *I have not found anyone willing to help me.* | 4% | 6% |
| *I do not know where to start.* | 5% | 7% |

| | | |
|---|---|---|
| My family members are not supportive. | 5% | 8% |
| My friends are not as interested in spiritual things. | 11% | 8% |
| I have other more important priorities right now. | 8% | 10% |
| I do not want to think about mistakes I have made in the past. | 10% | 12% |
| Spiritual growth will require a lot of hard work. | 16% | 13% |
| I do not want to get too personal with other people. | 9% | 15% |
| I have had bad past experiences with groups or individuals. | 9% | 16% |
| General busyness of life. | 23% | 22% [41] |

## Cultural Exegesis, Engagement and Discipleship

When considering the issue of discipleship in relation to culture, there are some important statistics the ministry leader must consider as a cultural exegete who desires to engage in contextualized discipleship. In response to the question "Are people growing?", thirty-eight percent of Christians say "they are happy with where they are in their spiritual life." When asked if they had made progress in their spiritual growth in the past year, forty percent of practicing Christians responded: "a lot" and fifty-one percent responded "some". Twenty percent of non-practicing Christians responded: "a lot" and forty-three percent said "some". The top three responses that were given by Christians who want to grow spiritually were as follows: Forty-three percent said they have a desire to know Jesus, or God, more; thirty-nine percent stated that it is important to be improving or growing in all things; thirty-five percent said they desire to be more like Jesus. However, only 1 in 5 Christians is involved in some sort of discipleship activity. Practicing and non-practicing Christians gave the following reasons when asked the question "What is standing in the way of such involvement?":

- I haven't found anyone willing to help me – 4%; 6%

- I don't know where to start – 5%; 7%

- My family members are not supportive – 5%; 8%

- My friends are not as interested in spiritual things – 11%; 8%

- I have other more important priorities right now – 8%; 10%

- I don't want to think about mistakes I've made in the past – 10%; 12%

- Spiritual growth will require a lot of hard work – 16%; 13%

- I don't want to get too personal with other people – 9%; 15%

- I've had bad past experiences with groups or individuals – 9%; 16%

- General busyness of life – 23%; 22%

The following statistics are based on the question "What is working with how Christians are discipled?" and are quite telling: 1 in 4 Christians is currently being discipled by someone; 1 in 5 Christians is discipling someone else, and 1 in 3 Christians is looking for one-on-one discipleship. Among the 9 out of 10 Christians who say that spiritual growth is important, their preference on how to be discipled is as follows: Thirty-seven percent - on their own; twenty-five percent - in a group; sixteen percent - one-on-one; and twenty-one percent - a mix of group + one-on-one.[42]

*Observations for Discipleship*

Three critical observations concerning discipleship are obvious from an exegesis of this and other contemporary cultural data. First, ministry leaders must emphasize to new Christian converts that the discipleship process is a necessary, lifelong journey. Second, ministry leaders cannot adhere to a one-size-fits-all model of the discipleship process. Third, more emphasis must be given to intergenerational discipleship. Adherence to these three observations will lead to a more robust and culturally contextualized discipleship process.

### Cultural Exegesis, Engagement and Ministry Leadership

When considering the issue of ministry leadership in relation to culture, it is imperative one realizes that what is considered effective leadership will differ from culture to culture. As a matter of fact, Baumgartner wrote that "these differences are not just interesting academic observations but are subtly present in the ways leaders are subjected to judgment by the often invisible yardsticks of values and expectations, and they indicate potential areas of conflict when leaders work with people of other cultures."[43] One significant research study on the relationship between cultural differences and leadership behaviors was the GLOBE study. In this study, nine cultural dimensions that influence leadership behavior and expectations were identified. These include assertiveness, institutional collectivism, in-group collectivism, future orientation, gender egalitarianism, humane orientation, performance orientation, power distance, and uncertainty avoidance. There were twenty-two universal positive leader attributes and three universal negative leader attributes identified; furthermore, there were thirty-five culturally contingent leader attributes.[44] These findings solidify the fact that there are universally desirable leadership attributes, but also that many desirable leadership attributes are contingent upon the cultural context.

Understanding the impact of culture upon ministry leadership,

Stetzer identified several needed leadership paradigm shifts that "values the discipleship core and priesthood of all believers as primary ministry drivers." These shifts included:

1. From Superman to everyone – an inclusive and gift-based ministry

2. From church to kingdom – a healthy focus on the broader sphere of God's reign

3. From 'me' to 'we' – a participatory involvement in ministry through teams

4. From personal power to people empowerment

5. From three tiers to one mission – mobilizing the multitudes to living out their faith

6. From "called to the ministry" to "called to ministry"

7. From "called to missions" to "sent on mission"

8. From "priests" to a "priesthood of believers"[45]

*Observations for Ministry Leadership*

Three critical observations concerning ministry leadership are obvious from an exegesis of this and other contemporary cultural data. First, the ministry leader must be open and willing to utilize various leadership styles according to cultural context. Second, a ministry leader must be a student of the culture in order to ascertain what leadership style is the most appropriate for this particular context. Third, the ministry leader must keep at the center of his leadership philosophy and practice a discipleship focus that equips followers who operate with a good faith that is culturally engaged.

## CONCLUSION

Culture is a much more complex issue than many ministry leaders consider it to be. Often, only the visible aspects of culture are taken into consideration when the unseen aspects of culture are actually the ones that have the most direct impact upon discipleship and ministry leadership. Therefore, it is of utmost importance for the ministry leader who desires to be the most effective in discipleship and leadership to develop a high level of cultural intelligence. As a result, this ministry leader will be better enabled to disciple believers and to lead followers toward faith contextualization and cultural engagement in a good faith manner.

Questions For Consideration

1. How does your current cultural context enhance and/or weaken age-graded ministry?

2. What are some intentional, intergenerational discipleship strategies you could develop to help foster cultural intelligence among the various generations in your context?

3. What are some ways that your ministry leader family can model cultural engagement in your particular context?

# CHAPTER 3

# EVANGELISM
## David Evans

*Although I am free from all and not anyone's slave, I have made myself a slave to everyone, in order to win more people.*
The Apostle Paul, 1 Corinthians 9: 19 (CSB)

## DEFINITION AND CHARACTERISTICS OF EVANGELISM

Evangelism, the belief that surrendered Christ followers should proclaim the Good News of Jesus Christ, is one of the main purposes of the church as mandated in the New Testament (Matthew 28:18-20, Luke 14:23, Acts 1:8). New Testament evangelism is considered to be "organic." The use of this word is not to spark popularity but clarity. For the sake of this chapter, "organic" means something that grows irregularly and acts naturally.

To begin, I will describe evangelism as "irregular" using the growth of a tree as an analogy. Each tree grows in a way that no other tree has grown. Each limb stretches in its own way to reach its goal of sunlight, thus, a tree grows irregularly. Just as there is not a set pattern for each tree to follow in growing, so evangelism does not have a set pattern for how the gospel is to be shared (Luke 9:2, 6; Acts 8:5, 9:20, 13:5, 15:35, 16:10). The timing and method of evangelism are irregular. If we are to be ambassadors of Christ, then we are to be ambassadors as often as we breathe. We cannot subdivide our time into segments of evangelism, discipleship, worship, prayer, family, recreation, sin, employment, and other areas. The Great Commission was designed to occur at every moment of our life (Matthew 28:20). This is not to mean that God does not bless efforts that are scheduled because I believe that He does bless scheduled efforts. New Testament evangelism occurs before, during, and after our scheduled efforts because we are called to be His ambassadors at all times (2 Corinthians 5:11-21).

New Testament evangelism is also "organic" because it is natural. The execution of evangelism is best processed through the experiences, abilities, and giftedness of the people within the church (2 Timothy 1: 8-12, 15-18). Evangelism is birthed through the empowerment of the Holy Spirit through the believers within the local church and is not fabricated (John 15:26, 16:7-11; 2 Timothy 1: 7). Lewis Drummond stated, "The Holy Spirit who seals us will also guide us."[46]

Methods of evangelism do not have a mold that fits every single body of Christ. To discover the best methods of evangelism the pastor must bridge the gap. The responsibility of the pastor is to hold onto the scope of the Scripture and implement it while examining the nuances of the particular body of Christ (2 Timothy 3:16). To discover the best evangelism methods of a particular local church, the pastor may not be able to buy a "box" from a store and apply it to the local church but instead may have to decipher how that local body "ticks" and design a Biblical method to the already existing cadence.

## HOW TO DESIGN AN EVANGELISTIC METHOD

Leading a church or small group to do evangelism can be daunting. Pre-existing models or no model at all may already be established. Designing a method that excites people is key. Excitement may sound trite, but why should ministry, especially evangelism, always be about doing something out of your comfort? Evangelistic methods can be created that attach to biblically accepted cadences of life. To look at the methods of evangelism, we must first look at a couple of assumptions that keep people from embracing evangelism.

*Two False Assumptions Concerning Evangelism*

An assumption is "a thing that is accepted as true or as certain to happen, without proof."[47] Two false assumptions concerning evangelism have stunted churches throughout the years. In the experience of the author, the following assumptions have been utilized as objections when a church attempts to carry out an evangelistic program/process: (1) evangelism as personality-driven, (2) and evangelism as a spiritual gift.

First, evangelism is not personality-driven but is rather Spirit-driven (John 15:26, 16:7-11; 2 Timothy 1:7). Most people believe that people with an over-the-top personality must be designed to be evangelists. Although some evangelists have an over-the-top personality, not all evangelists are relegated to such a characteristic. If personality dictates the evangelistic calling or effectiveness, then personality is what empowers the evangelistic movement. Francis Chan stated,

> "Even our church growth can happen without Him. Let's be honest: If you combine a charismatic speaker, a talented worship band, and some hip, creative events, people will attend your church. Yet this does not mean that the Holy Spirit of God is actively working and moving in the lives of the people who are coming. It simply means that you have created a space that is appealing enough to draw people in for an hour or two on Sunday."[48]

The Bible teaches that an evangelistic movement is the plan and purpose of God unto His creation thus empowered by the Holy Spirit and not personality (John 14: 26, Acts 8: 26-40).[49] If we hold that evangelism is Spirit-driven and we believe that the Holy Spirit dwells within all followers of Christ, then we must hold that evangelism is a mission and purpose for every follower of Christ. In other words, the Holy Spirit indwells all followers of Christ to be His ambassadors and to give witness of His greatness (2 Corinthians 5:20; Ephesians 6:20; Matthew 28: 18-20; Acts 1:8).

Second, evangelism is not a spiritual gift.[50] If evangelism is a spiritual gift, then we must accept that there are those that are designed to be better at evangelism and are only part of the ecclesiological process. If evangelism is not a gift but rather an office, then it would make sense that it be led by particular people and mandated to everyone. In other words, evangelism as a spiritual gift is the responsibility of part of the body; whereas, evangelism as an office is the responsibility of everyone led by particular people. The office of an evangelist is that of a leader who equips the saints and assists the whole church to engage the community with the Gospel.

Let me contend with you that evangelism is not a spiritual gift (Rom. 12:6-8; 1 Cor.12:4-11; 1 Pet. 4: 10-11). A gift is a treasure given to a select group, but evangelism is a command for all Christ followers. Thus, evangelism is not a gift but an expectation and mandate of those who follow Christ. As a pastor, I have heard it said that since evangelism was not a gift of a certain person then he or she would not have to be evangelistic. Examining scripture shows us that the word "evangelism" does not appear. The word "evangelist" appears three times (Acts 21:8, Eph.4:11 and 2 Tim.4:5). In each of the usages, the word "evangelist" is utilized as a position or office, not a gift.

*Evangelism as Process*

Throughout my years in ministry, I have seen the Southern Baptist denomination inundated with "one size fits all" evangelism strategies for a Great Commission fulfillment.[51] Many strategies have championed several aspects of evangelism and have served great purposes throughout the church. However, most programs attempt to be a mold to fit everyone. Sadly, at times a leader may feel the pressure to do anything to keep the program alive. As a leader continues to fuel the program with people, the people get burned out and question the genuine motives and the program's effectiveness. It is easy to get lost in the program and forget about evangelism.[52] On the other hand, the purpose of a process is to identify key characteristics of a particular group and evolve as the group grows. A problem with programs is the shelf life, whereas, processes evolve. The process embraces one method of faithfully explaining and applying the Gospel message but may use many applications to accomplish the one goal.[53]

In 1877, Lottie Moon developed a mission strategy that matched her passion, calling and context. She was most comfortable with an educational approach to sharing the gospel, but deemed fit to change methods and "work quietly within her own neighborhood."[54] To personalize an evangelistic process involves ingenuity. Unfortunately, ingenuity seems to be a lost art. There was a day that men and women would gather to find a solution when a problem arose and press forward to see the solution come to fruition. People would blaze new trails in life with the hopes of finding new solutions to problems. At times, a solution would not solve the problem but would instead lead to another "link" in the solution chain. This "link" would allow people to have something to embrace for a season until they were able to graduate to the next phase of the process. How do ingenuity and evangelism relate? Evangelistic solutions cannot be found in a mold produced away from the specific local church. Copying another church's model or plan does not necessarily solve a church's lack of evangelism.

A. W. Tozer stated:

> "We may as well face it: the whole level of spirituality among us is low. We have measured ourselves by ourselves until the incentive to seek higher plateaus in the things of the Spirit is all but gone ... (We) have imitated the world, sought popular favor, manufactured delights to substitute for the joy of the Lord and produced a cheap and synthetic power to substitute for the power of the Holy Ghost."[55]

# DEVELOPING AN EVANGELISM MODEL

Is it possible that as a church leader, the Lord has assigned you at this outpost for the purpose of blazing a new trail? Maybe your job is to discover an evangelistic method that is tailor-made for your congregation. Honestly, you must ask yourself, if the Lord wanted you to do the same exact evangelism methods as the church down the road, then why does He need your congregation? I believe that there is a method that He has called you and only you to do.

Ingenuitive evangelism involves finding the most efficient way to be "Great Commissioned" people in a community. It is not necessarily creating a new method but finding a new path in an already existing cadence of life for church people and community. The cadence of life could be a cadence that members of the church already enjoy or one that the community commonly accepts. Why is the cadence important? When developing an evangelism strategy (a church approach to glorifying God by seeing people surrender their life to Jesus while strategically going against the gates of hell) the path of least resistance may be the easiest way to get the strategy started. You will have enough struggles without choosing to embrace some unnecessary problems. The goal is to discover and implement the best model and method for the congregation and the local community to embrace and receive.

First, study the culture of your church and your community and find the aspects that excite them (service project, hobby, fellowship activity, etc.) or spheres of life for which people already live (work, school, recreation, hobby, etc.).[56] Second, prayerfully consider and construct an evangelistic ministry plan that you can connect with the exciting aspect or sphere of life. Ask the following questions: (1) How can these people be Great Commissioned people when they complete this task that they already enjoy? (2) What value can we bring to the community through this project and will the community be excited if we are there? Russell Moore stated, "The gospel is also social, reconciling people with one another, and motivating them to care for human flourishing and human suffering."[57]

Is ingenuitive evangelism biblical? Paul wrote to the church at Corinth that they were to become all things to all men (join existing cadences) as to reach them with the Gospel:

> [19] *Although I am free from all and not anyone's slave, I have mad myself a slave to everyone, in order to win more people.* [20] *To the Jews I became like a Jew, to win Jews; to those under the Law, like one under the Law –though I myself am not under the law—to win those under the law.* [21] *To those who are without the law, like one without the law—though I am not without God's law but under under the law of Christ— to win those without law.* [22] *To the weak I became weak, in order to win the weak; I have become all things to all people, so that I may by every possible means save some.* [23] *Now I do all this because of the gospel, so that I may share in the blessings. 1 Corinthians 9:19-23, CSB*

In the Bible, we see men and women uniquely designed by God to do ministry (Psalm 139:13-14; Isa. 64:8; Matt. 10:29-31; Rom. 9:21; 1 Thess. 1: 6; 1 Pet. 2:9; 2 Pet. 1: 5-9). God chose to express His love and will through human beings (Luke 19:36-40). The men and women communicating God's glory to others are not drawn back to an identical program but an identical purpose. Although the goal of purpose is the same, the methods for completing the purpose do not necessitate an identical mold. In other words, evangelism has one purpose but many methods to complete the same goal. The methods of evangelism are adaptable and contextual.

Throughout my years as a pastor, I have found that evangelism methods revolving around something as fun and exciting as personal hobbies tend to be easily implemented and received. As you find a place that excites a certain demographic in your church, namely a hobby, then attempt to connect it with a ministry.

For example, if you have someone in your church that is a hunter or fisherman then you may have an opportunity to rid yourself of a typical benevolence ministry. Instead of handing out monies and groceries to the next person that randomly calls the church, you could have an intentional evangelism process in place that could reach hurting people in your community. Buy a deep freezer, then get the hunters or fishermen to fill it up for the church. By the way, most of the hunters and fishermen that I know are looking for ways to go hunting and fishing more because their personal freezers are full. If you give them an opportunity to fill the church's freezer full of meat, then that by itself will attract hunters and fishermen to your church. When someone calls you will then have food to give to him or her. If the hunters or fishermen are similar to the ones that I know, then they are going to be protective of the meat and would prefer to hand it out themselves. Go ahead and let them. It would be one less thing that the pastoral staff will have to do. Each hunter and fisherman also takes pride in how it is cooked and, for the most part, will teach others how to cook the meat that they caught. This tactic may allow a church member to be invited into a home in the community, build a relationship, and be one step closer to presenting the gospel. Such a story has worked out in many local churches, essentially growing a force of unassuming hunters and fishermen to become evangelists. Randy Davis, the Executive Director of the Tennessee Baptist Mission Board, stated: "What if we do not classify success on who comes but who goes?"[58]

*Here is a "Pep Talk" –*

When you attempt to blaze new paths, be prepared for failure. The outcome of failing is most often dependent on your outlook on life. If you are a pessimist, then you will be swallowed by the negativity involved in the failure. If you are an optimist, then you will struggle to accept the failing as negative. Failing innately is neither negative nor positive but an opportunity for change. You will be able to utilize it as a stepping-stone or stumbling block. Failing does not have to set a negative stigma but could be a welcoming place for people that are failing in life and are struggling to see success themselves. You could consider a healing pattern for those in your community to help them realize that life and great opportunity exist after failure. Does the failure excite you or does it depress you?

As you carry your calling out as an evangelistic scientist, attempting to find the best models and methods that fit your local church and community, you will experience many failures. Just know that with each failure, you are just one step closer to success. In the meantime, while you are trying your best to set a scene for Great Commission influence, you are sowing seeds in everyone involved in the process. Sowing Great Commissioned seeds in people's lives is necessary to replant vision, mission, and structure. Chuck Kelly, the President of the New Orleans Baptist Theological Seminary, stated, "Southern Baptists are a harvest-oriented denomination living in the midst of an unseeded generation."[59]

## HOW TO MEASURE AN EVANGELISTIC DISCIPLE MAKING PROGRAM/PROCESS

When considering an evangelism method, a measuring tool will add objectivity. Whether you are considering a new or repeated method, a measuring tool is necessary. The Evangelistic Metric and Measurement Assessment Scale (EMMA) is a value rubric for pre-discipleship programs. The rubric measures the value of considered evangelistic programs and processes. The purpose of the measuring value is to assess if the necessary evangelistic elements are present in the program. The rubric consists of two processes: (1) a pre-program measurement, and (2) a post-program measurement.

The Evangelistic Metric and Measurement
Assessment Scale (EMMA) Scale

| Pre-Program/Process Evaluation (to consider if program should begin) | | |
|---|---|---|
| Value | | Category |
| "1" | – | **Identify** - The program/process identifies lost people. |
| "1" | – | **Equip** - The program/process equips the church to reach lost people. |
| "2" | – | **Engage** - The program/process engages lost people. |
| If a program "identifies" and "equips" then its value is "2," if a program only "identifies" then it is given the value of "1." | | |
| Post-Program/Process Evaluation (to consider if program should continue) | | |
| Value | | Category |
| "3" – **Survey** – A measurement for those that participated in the program/process. The measurement assists the church leadership when determining if the outcome of the program/process rises to the level of evangelistic disciple making process necessary for being a church. Each answer is worth a particular value. The values are: "1" = 0; "2" = 0.25; "3" = 0.50; "4" = 1. If a participant answers each question by circling the number "4" then the participant will receive an overall score/value of "3". | | |
| **A SAMPLE Quantitative Research Survey** | | |
| 1. How many times have you shared the Gospel or had a Gospel conversation with someone since the conference/event/training? <br>     1. 0      2. 1-4      3. 5-10      4. 11 or more | | |
| 2. How many hours have you spent teaching someone else the principles that you learned from the conference/event/training? <br>     1. 0      2. 1-4      3. 5-10      4. 11 or more | | |

3. How many times have you prayed for lost people around you since the conference/event/training?

    1. 0       2. 1-4       3. 5-10       4. 11 or more

### Total Score

_____(Pre-Program Score)

+_____(Post-Program Score)

=_____(Total Score)

**"0-7" total value of a program.**

The pre-program measurement assesses if the program/process identifies people groups, evangelistically equips the saints, or engages a people group with the Gospel. If the program identifies people groups in your area, then it receives a score of "1". If the program equips the saints to share the Gospel with the community, then it receives a score of "1". If the program engages a person or a people group with the Gospel, then it receives a score of "2". A total of "4" points are available to assess the program/process before it launches.

*Pre-program Measurement*

The pre-program measurement occurs before the program/process has occurred and in most cases can occur before anyone else knows that it is being considered. For example, a church that is considering another year of Vacation Bible School (VBS) can use the EMMA Scale to evaluate the performance of the program as not to leave out any necessary evangelistic elements for a healthy discipleship process. Through the years of operation, your church's use of a VBS program may have overlooked certain principles that made it an effective evangelism strategy. The VBS program should not necessarily be sacrificed because of the lack of the element. If the church includes the one element, then VBS may regain the evangelistic/disciple-making vigor that it once had. Why is that a win? For most churches, VBS is an annual ministry with a dedicated core of volunteers. VBS has been a natural fit for so many churches that it is an easy sell. In fact, many churches use VBS as a selling point to start Backyard Kids Clubs, which are more evangelistic.

*Post-program Measurement*

The post-program measurement is a survey that assesses if the program/process has the desired outcome. The survey assesses Gospel conversations, reproducibility and evangelistic prayer. The survey is to be administered after the program/process. Each participant will be surveyed to measure if principles taught affected lostness. The survey distributed within 1-6 months of program/process (TABLE 1). The survey will score on percentages based on the success of each question. The participant will need to choose one of the four multiple-choice options. Each answer is worth a particular value. The values are as follows: $1 = 0$; $2 = 0.25$; $3 = 0.50$; $4 = 1$. If a participant answers "4" for each question then the participant will receive an overall score/value of "3", as each "4" is valued 1. You will then add the overall score/value of the survey (in this case it is "3") with the overall score given during the Pre-Program/Process Evaluation and that will be your total score of evangelistic effectiveness for that program or process for that individual. To measure the overall evangelistic effectiveness for an entire group, add up the overall score values from all the collected surveys and divide that result by the number of participants. This will give you the average score of the survey and allow you to add it to the overall score from the Pre-Program/Process Evaluation.

"Total Score" will objectively describe the evangelistic disciple making value of the program or process. The score will do one of two things: (1) affirm that the program/process is effective in evangelism and discipleship; (2) or identify general areas of need when considering an evangelistic program that effectively makes disciples.

*The Results of the EMMA Scale*

If the value assessed is acceptable, then the EMMA Scale's value is to provide a scheduled review of the program to provide insight if the program continues to be of value. If the value assessed is unacceptable, then consider allowing someone to review the program through the EMMA Scale and compare results. If the results are similar and elements are obviously absent then consider the process for creating an innovative evangelistic process or adding evangelistic elements to the current program or process of evangelism. If abandoning the current program or process of evangelism is not an option or is not in the best interest of the church and community, then consider adding absent elements to the program or process. When adding evangelistic elements to a program or process, a church can begin with a few options: (1) read materials on the particular issues, (2) consider helps from the denomination, and (3) inquire from local pastoral leaders. The author has always found that all three considerations are key when determining the best fit for the local church and community.
Questions for Personal Reflection:

1. Name the people that you know that are not Christians. What do you do to get to know the non-Christians in your area? What do you need to do to hang out with non-Christians more?

2. How often do you pray for non-Christians?[60] How often do you serve them as to show them Christ's love? When do you plan to share the gospel with them?

3. When was the last time that you attempted to share the gospel? When was the last time that you inspected (reviewed, criticized or scrutinized) your personal methods of evangelism? Are you more effective in your approach or less effective? What elements can you add that will make you a better witness of Christ?

4. What can you do to help your church (faith family) better evangelistic communications? How can you do this in an edifying manner?

5. Who is mentoring you to be a better witness of Christ? What books are you reading? What sermons are you listening to? Who is discipling you to be a better witness?

## CHAPTER 4

# MENTORING

## Jody Dean

"Live your life passionately for God, not your own agenda, your own promotion, or your own good. This is not advice to burn out, but it is to burn up! It's really great to see what the Lord is doing in your life."

-Words from one of my mentors early in my ministry

**Personal Story**

My life changed in a dramatic way due to the investment of a more devoted Christian disciple in my life over a season of twenty-one years and counting. When I think back over the years of my journey, the common theme is a strategic investment by people into my life. Some of these people were teachers of the Bible, some mentors to everyday life issues, and others a field guide to an area of my life. These three components together with the utilization of the spiritual disciplines, the work of the Holy Spirit, and the vital connection to a local body of believers created a pathway for me to be discipled.

## Biblical Examples

People serving as field guides for others in the faith that are younger in age or maturity are interwoven throughout the scriptures. A mentor can sometimes be found within your family. Moses' father-in-law Jethro sharing advice in regard to governing and dealing with the people is one family example in the Bible. Another example of family mentorship concerns Naomi and Ruth and how they cared for one another. Joseph was tormented and sold into slavery for being the favored son, but as God worked and moved in Joseph's life, a transformation to mentor and provide for his entire family is presented. Mentors can also be found through everyday life as we observe Jesus calling ordinary men to be his disciples and within ministry relationships like the one between Paul and Timothy.

Since my call to ministry came in high school and my serving in the local church as a minister began at eighteen, I appreciate the relationship between Paul and Timothy. In each of these relationships, we see a leader who chose to make a significant investment into someone else whether a family member, fellow disciple, or leader. We all have common ways as Christians to find community through our family, work or friends and through those that mentor us. As you begin to think about your life, who in your family can you mentor, or who could mentor you? In your work relationships and friendships, who could you make a significant investment in as a mentor? Is there a leader in your life that you would like to learn from as an apprentice? Do you find yourself at a place where you could have an apprentice or intern underneath your leadership? In the following pages, we will examine the need to mentor and be mentored as we explore scriptural examples that reveal the need to invest into others to for kingdom impact.

An example of an amazing relationship in the Gospels is between Jesus and Peter. Peter was an ordinary man who left everything in order to be inquisitive with Jesus. Peter tried to diligently comprehend and discern the meaning and disconnect that he encountered during intimate moments when Jesus shared major insights into the kingdom.

He was the first disciple whom Jesus called (Matthew 4). In Matthew chapter 8, Jesus made a huge impact in Peter's family by healing a family member. Peter tried to walk on water, but just as you and I do, he became distracted by his circumstances and his focus on Jesus waned. We see Jesus, the mentor, allowing Peter to speak rashly and overreach in his ambitions, but he also encouraged his mentees.

During a storm on the sea, Jesus asked some thought-provoking questions to Peter and the other disciples in the boat to reveal to them their limited faith. I have been on a lake when an unexpected storm rolled in, and it can be frightening. I can imagine the immediate fear the disciples felt as a storm was tossing the boat and the water became more treacherous. I have always marveled that Peter was the only disciple who asked to leave the boat and join Jesus on the water in the midst of a storm in which one would not typically want to leave the vessel.

Another encounter with Jesus and his disciples is found in Matthew 15 when Peter asked a question which led to another hard question like during the stormy sea encounter. At this point, you might wonder if the other disciples want Peter to stop asking so many questions. However, in a mentoring relationship, open communication and seeking answers to questions should be an integral part of the relationship. As a mentor, you should allow for questions and treat the mentee with grace.

Peter also struggled at times as the mentee and even made great mistakes as he was discipled by Jesus. It can be difficult to grasp that Peter's denial of Jesus and Christ's response to Peter after the resurrection would qualify him to lead the church forward. We see a true picture of investing and staying with someone through the "thick and thin," trusting the Lord to work in a mentee or mentor's life. I have benefited over the years from mentors that stuck by me through various aspects of life and ministry. Jesus provided the best example for a mentor to stay loyal to their disciples through life. Jesus even let Judas remain with the group until his decisions ultimately ended his life.

Paul and Timothy's relationship has always encouraged me in my journey to be more like Christ. Their relationship of mentoring for ministry multiplication is my experience. I believe that a mentor should encourage you in your walk with Christ, help you understand the culture in which you are living, be a guide for cultivating spiritual disciplines, and help you as you navigate being deployed to serve. I believe mentoring is crucial in your family, minister, volunteer, business, and church life. Paul invested his life and ministry into Timothy, and Timothy, in turn, did the same with others. The unique component that we should not lose is the discipline to cultivate a culture of discipleship. This culture begins in mentoring relationships that are a catalyst for being part of group life in a church as well as part of the crowd that gathers to worship or even the larger crowd we interact within society each day.

Another crucial component for mentoring that we can learn from the Apostle Paul is that he mentored people for life. He did not do it for just a semester or a few years, but he invested in people his entire life by writing and encouraging them. Even more important than being an encouragement for your mentees is being a prayer warrior to God on their behalf. Paul shared in the beginning of his letters that he prayed for the believers he was addressing. A good example of Paul praying for his mentees is found in Philippians. He wrote, "I give thanks to my God for every remembrance of you, always praying with joy for all of you in my every prayer, because of your partnership in the gospel from the first day until now. I am sure of this, that he who started a good work in you will carry it on to completion until the day of Jesus Christ." (Phil. 1: 3-6, CSB) As you reflect on Paul's words, do you have the same testimony of praying and thanking God for those close in the ministry who work with you?

In his book on mentoring, Bobb Biehl wrote: "Mentoring is a lifelong relationship, in which a mentor helps a protégé reach her or his God-given potential."[61] The concept of an apprentice or mentor is not unique to the church. We find mentorship in business, education, medicine, and trade throughout history and society. The scriptures teach us that more mature believers should disciple others. The term mentoring is fitting based on the examples of people given who invest in family and friends for the purpose of gospel advancement. Mentoring has come to mean anything from a cup of coffee at Starbucks to catch up on life to a professor chairing the committee of a doctoral student. Although the term is widely used within and without ministry circles, specific clarity should be determined for each of us as we seek mentoring relationships as part of our lives.

## CULTIVATING MENTORING RELATIONSHIPS

Some people have a definite period of time for a mentoring relationship to start and stop. These can range from one semester, one year, or several years. These predetermined lengths for a mentoring relationship can mirror the specific three-year period the disciples walked with Jesus. However, Paul revealed a lifelong commitment in his writing to continue to speak truth and encouragement into partners in the ministry. Life circumstances can also determine the length of a mentoring relationship, such as moving to another city, life events with family, or shifting your focus for the health of the relationship. Though distance separated Paul from people, he wrote to encourage and mentor as well as continue to pray for them.

The terms and relationships are varied in my life. I have had people in my life for a season that is a beneficial relationship for that season. We would pray together, encourage one another, and help to develop one another in specific areas of life. Another aspect of mentoring is connecting to those who are in your life for a set amount of time due to the nature of your work. The idea of having an intern for a set amount of time to learn about a specific area of work is common. Many college students prepare for their career by interning in the field which they are studying. Churches and Parachurch ministries have utilized summer staffing and internships as structured mentoring opportunities to develop people as they sense a desire to be more connected to ministry or are praying about vocational ministry. Although these types of mentoring are needed and impact lives, the life-long commitment to be involved in a mentees life should be the standard we all strive to achieve.

Many years ago Biehl clarified that mentoring was not evangelism, discipleship, or modeling. I would also add leadership to that list. In recent years, Christians have blurred the lines between terms which has caused us to expect results that cannot be derived when we are not clear in what we are striving to accomplish. Mentoring should provide a personal relationship with a coach who can help a person achieve their potential. Todd Wilson wrote, "One-on-one coaching is a critical piece of our journey. It amplifies the discovery and effectiveness of calling."[62] The mentors that still invest in my life today have accomplished exactly what Wilson stated by helping me to further discover my calling and live it out effectively. The short-term mentoring relationships in my life did not achieve the same level of effectiveness. Mentoring relationships that are not ongoing will fade in their effectiveness for the duration of the journey. Imagine setting out on a long journey with key people who help you stay focused and on course for a short time, then choose to exit from your life as opposed to continuing to walk through life together. I am thankful that my life-long mentors did not choose to exit from my life, but chose to still serve as a guide and faithful example to continue the journey of life together.

Mentors also make mistakes that strain a relationship. A mentoring relationship should serve as an accountability standard to stay committed to our relationship with Christ. A committed mentor that walks with Christ will find it more difficult to keep unconfessed sin in his or her life. When you think of accountability, it is not simply asking the question of how things are going. Accountability should dive deep by asking the difficult questions. I believe this should be a reciprocal dialogue in the mentoring relationship.

Jesus modeled the ongoing commitment to mentor others during the journey with his disciples. He continued to cultivate these men by being an example, providing accountability and encouragement for the journey, giving responsibility, and filling in the voids of their understanding. Jesus modeled a strategic relationship with his disciples that allowed them to pursue the journey. A mentoring relationship should involve living life together.

Sharing life together can be a challenge since letting people into our lives can be difficult. My family is the easiest component to mentoring in regard to sharing life. They see me at my best and my worst. My wife and I are accountable to one another and strive to mentor one another and our children to be more like Christ. However, it can be a struggle to let people outside of our home be close enough to see us at anything but our best. However, the in-depth relationships of Jesus with his twelve disciples, Paul and Timothy, and Peter with the leaders of the early church reveal more than a casual church relationship where they just greeted each other when they gathered to worship.

The culture shift of coming home to escape from the day has been a shift from sitting on the porch and playing in the front yard that was my childhood. Yet, people are more connected than ever today through social media by seeing pictures and knowing the activities of family, friends, associates, neighbors, and acquaintances. As you begin to reflect on your practices of sharing life with others, what does it look like in your weekly rhythm? Do you resonate with the harsh truth that you desire not to see more people as you conclude your day? Andy Stanley and Bob Willits wrote that "The last thing you want to do is have one more conversation, be forced to make one more decision, or fulfill one more request. Our goal is to avoid people—and what they potentially want from us—at all cost!"[63] While American society has built the reality of loneliness, it is Bonhoeffer who provided a counter to this reality:

> "Every man is called separately and must follow alone. But men are frightened of solitude, and they try to protect themselves in the society of their fellow-men and in their material environment. They become suddenly aware of their responsibilities and duties and are loath to part with them. But all this is only a cloak to protect them from having to make a decision. They are unwilling to stand alone before Jesus and to be compelled to decide with their eyes fixed on him alone."[64]

So we must make a resolution about how to balance the individual personal relationship with Christ and the need for community to share our life. A mentoring relationship is a great way to begin sharing your life and thus to begin establishing Christian community.

As we read in the Gospels, we see Jesus begin to move from the crowds to the disciples in his ministry. Each of us needs the individual relationship in which we interact on a one-on-one level. We also need a more intimate core group which expands to a larger small group to ultimately impact the crowds around us. This inverted funnel of relationships begins by each of us being the individual disciple we have been called to be who then moves to impact others. Imagine the impact on the church as we begin to share our lives with others as Jesus did. Our personal responsibility in the Great Commission begins to unfold for a kingdom impact as we are deployed using our gifts and investing into other people.

Time is a component to investing that cannot be hijacked. Financial advisors will tell you that there are no shortcuts to a lifetime of saving and investing. Each paycheck commitment pays off after many decades of being strategic to save and invest and then the momentum continues. Mentoring relationships that look to the long-term view of a lifetime will see a similar momentum as saving and investing. A short-term mentoring relationship will reveal limited fruit. The time commitment in a rushed and frazzled world can be a challenge. I see this each semester in academics as people strive to finish coursework. Discipline and time management seem to be crucial for completing most tasks that we commit to accomplish.

I believe our struggle in discipleship is similar to business. We get overwhelmed with the vast idea of reaching a lost world for Christ in addition to helping each other become more like Him. In a company, effectiveness is diluted when everyone tries to handle everything. Mentoring takes away a corporate approach to discipleship, but it requires a strategic investment of time. These types of relationships are more organic and cannot be programmed or easily administered by a third party through a church office.

Time is one resource that is equal among all disciples. Each person has 1,440 minutes a day to spend. If you sleep an average of seven hours a day and then subtract 420 minutes, the remaining 1,020 minutes is left for each of us to manage and invest with a kingdom mindset. We each have fixed responsibilities from home, work, church, and hobbies that we schedule and maintain. I believe we can also find time to invest in mentoring another person.

## SERVING THE LORD THROUGH MENTORING RELATIONSHIPS

Mentoring is a much-needed part of our service unto the Lord. The level you get to know each other, the life coaching, and the changing stages of life and devotion bring to light the need to have someone a little further along in the journey who mentors the next generation of disciples. I do not believe this should be an age factor, but rather, a component of spiritual maturity. However, I have benefited greatly when my mentor was both older and more spiritually mature.

People always make time for what they value, such as a TV show or sporting event. Mentoring should naturally fit into a rhythm in the Christian's life. The natural component has to be a part of this process. In the church, we must encourage and promote the need for mentoring and let people begin to see the fruit of and desire to serve as mentors for others. We must help people understand that mentoring relationships are more informal and we must be willing to remove barriers. Do you intentionally seek out people that you discern have potential and invite them to a strategic mentoring relationship? I have a personal policy to mentor men only. I believe mentoring relationships for many reasons need to remain personal and detailed in a way that could be inappropriate if it was co-ed. Jesus had other relationships with disciples, smaller groups of people, and crowds.

A mentoring relationship is a special interaction that requires the right connection among the participants. Do not be discouraged if a mentoring relationship does not work out. We see several encounters in scripture that caused people to split or go another direction. As this happens, respond with grace and help them to move on. Then, seek out another disciple who you can help on their journey.

Mentoring relationships can be messy and time-consuming. When you invest in others, sometimes people decide to take a different route than the advice you gave. Since many of us have been stubborn at one time or another, it is important to remember that we are in the process of sanctification to be more like Christ. We have not arrived and people sin and make mistakes. I know in years past I have not always taken all the advice I have been given. Sometimes it was good discernment that although the advice was solid, God intended something different, but, most of the time, I should have listened to my mentor.

Sometimes the mentee will make mistakes or desire to end the relationship. Jesus knew someone would betray him from his core group of disciples. He kept all twelve and continued to follow the Father all the way to the Cross. You and I probably share the desire to discover who is against us. We cannot get sidetracked by all the things that can go wrong in mentoring relationships, but we must consider parameters for your mentoring relationships.

Jesus stayed steadfast to the work to which He was called. I believe we can see parameters as he withdrew from crowds and was alone at times in the garden or away from the group asleep on the boat. He also had to rebuke the disciples at certain times due to conversations, questions, or actions. I believe the blessing of being able to mentor others far out outweighs any negatives that could occur.

In a mentoring relationship, I would encourage you to keep a pulse on a few aspects of the Christian life as you invest in mentoring relationships. First, find a disciple that is striving to grow in Christ and is willing to go to a deeper level in their relationship and commitment. I would find a pathway that ensures that you are growing in the Word together. The Bible is the best place to discover true principles for our lives and should be foundational to a mentoring relationship. You need to be sure that the spiritual disciplines are incorporated into the time spent together. It is easy to spend your time catching up on life and activity and not spend as much time in prayer or components of spiritual formation. As your relationship continues to develop, look for ways to grow in ministry involvement. Sometimes we have people serving in our ministries and a mentoring relationship naturally emerges. The reality is that this is not always the case, and many times a mentor must be intentional in their leadership to seek out a mentee. A good mentor will also exhibit qualities that a mentee wants to emulate. Paul reminded us of this in 1 Corinthians, "I am not writing this to shame you, but to warn you as my dear children. For you may have countless instructors in Christ, but you don't have many fathers. For I became your father in Christ Jesus through the gospel. Therefore, I urge you, to imitate me. This is why I have sent Timothy to you. He is my dearly loved and faithful child in the Lord. He will remind you about my ways in Christ Jesus, just as I teach everywhere in every church." (1 Cor. 4: 14-17 CSB)

Questions for Reflection

My prayer for you as you continue to read this book is that you will commit to living a life like Paul that, if modeled, will look like Christ. A high goal for each of us would be to have spiritual children like Paul had in Timothy and others that could look to a man with a thorn in his flesh and see the example of a life devoted to Christ. Will you take a few moments and consider your life and what may need to change to be the example you have been called to be for Christ? Also, spend some time praying for God to lead you to someone to invest in as a mentor if you do not do so already. If you have a mentor, pray for them now. If you are mentoring someone currently, then pray for them.

## CHAPTER 5

# SMALL GROUPS

## Eddie Mosley

## INTRODUCTION

Small groups can help life change happen through studying the Bible, serving others, building community, and practicing accountability. The focus of small groups is not just about getting through a Bible study, but about striving to see a transformation take place in people's lives helping people accomplish goals. And many times, leaders are developed through a small group ministry by using an intentional process.

Few things in life help us grow to reach our goals, as does a group of close friends who walk with us through the good times and the bad. This group of friends joins us on the journey of life to accomplish goals through the crises of life. The Weight-Watchers program has them. Support groups practice them. Successful teams understand how to benefit from them. The first church had them, and even Jesus had one. God did not design us to live in isolation.

Approaches, definitions, and expectations for small groups vary from church to church, but the command found in Matthew is still the same: "Go, therefore, and make disciples of all nations, baptizing them in the name of the Father and of the Son and of the Holy Spirit, teaching them to observe everything I have commanded you. And remember, I am with you always, to the end of the age." (Matthew

28:19-20 CSB) The early church in Acts realized that doing life together produces disciples,

"They devoted themselves to the apostles' teaching, to the fellowship, to the breaking of bread, and to prayer. Everyone was filled with awe, and many wonders and signs were being performed through the apostles. Now all the believers were together and held all things in common. They sold their possessions and property and distributed the proceeds to all, as any had need. Every day they devoted themselves to meeting together in the temple, and broke bread from house to house. They ate their food with joyful and sincere hearts, praising God and enjoying the favor with all the people. Every day the Lord added to their number those who were being saved." (Acts 2:42-47 CSB)

Matthew 28 and Acts 2 provide a picture of how the church should look. These scriptures provide some of the foundations for small groups whether a group meets on Sunday mornings or during the week, in a home or the church building. The story in these verses begins with teaching, not with enlisting nor with leadership training sessions. The story is about evangelizing the lost, spending time together, caring for one another, helping to disciple each other, and spending time in worship. Small groups have an opportunity to practice these today just like the early church's first small groups. This chapter will help you discover how small groups help enable us to follow Jesus, experience life transformation and help others do the same.

In a small group setting, people study the Bible together and discuss the issues and challenges of life. They pray and care for one another, and someone in the group typically notices if another person does not attend. The results are close friendships. Organic in nature, small groups can transform a large church into a small, intimate congregation. Margaret Mead, at one time the most famous anthropologist in the world, said, "Never doubt that a small group of thoughtful, committed citizens can change the world; indeed, it's the only thing that ever has."[65]

What does this small group process look like in real life? Perhaps my personal story will help to answer this question. When my family and I moved into a new home in a new city, we quickly discovered that our neighbors were not excited about a preacher moving in next door. Because of past experiences, ministers were, in their mind, judgmental people. Their experiences in the church were not happy memories. They had attended church as kids, but, soon after getting married, they left the church and began to live as many Americans do, chasing the American dream. They had established friendships with many of the neighbors. They were a friendly and outgoing couple, even hosting weekly or monthly fellowship nights at their house.

Months went by with little more than waving or saying hello over the back fence. Unlike privacy fences, we had forty-two-inch high picket fences, which enabled conversations to take place across the backyards. As we talked, jobs would come up in conversation, but they would typically change the subject when my role as a minister entered the conversation. We invited them several times to a cookout, dessert party, and even a small group gathering in our home. The typical response was "No; thank you, though". We did not give up, however. We were neighbors and saw each other every weekend and several evenings during the week. Over the years, these neighbors became great friends of ours. We helped each other with lawn work, cleaning gutters, and taking care of each other's pets, but never discussed church. We continued to invite them to our small group meetings or cookouts. Their answers continued to grow more precise until they finally asked, "Is this event for the neighborhood or church? If it is for the church, we will send a pie. If it is for the neighborhood, we will bring a pie." That was the beginning of a beautiful disciple-making relationship.

Four years into our relationship with our neighbors, they finally came to one of our small group cookouts. Larry was a manager of a local warehouse. A man who was aware of Christ, but had no relationship with Jesus Christ. His wife was a homemaker, excellent cook, and one of the most caring women you could ever meet. They were neighborly but unchurched. Larry and his wife began to attend our neighborhood small group and soon grew to be close friends with everyone in the group. Two years after they initially attended the small group, they became followers of Christ and were baptized. After that, they never missed a small group meeting and even shared from their own life stories. They continued to grow and, in two more years, Larry started co-leading our small group. His comments in group meetings usually centered around the unchurched at his work, prayer requests which his co-workers had shared with him, or concern for an employee that he counseled during the previous week. Conversations before and after the formal small group Bible study helped him to understand what it meant to be an example at work and in the neighborhood. Today, his impact as a disciple is reaching far beyond the church walls. He employs men who have struggled financially and ethically, is known as a prayer warrior, and shares daily from his personal Bible study time. His wife spends time each week praying for and assisting the underprivileged kids and struggling families. The small group has had a life-changing impact on this couple and on those whom God has called them to serve and reach for His Kingdom.

## HOW SMALL GROUPS ENABLE TRANSFORMATION

### Evangelism

Jesus' invitation found in Matthew 4:19 gives a clear process for making disciples: "Follow me... I will make you fishers for people."[66] In this short verse, Jesus lays out a process of evangelism, discipleship, and multiplication. Small groups can be a vital part of this transformational process. This verse gives instruction on how a new convert can grow into a Christian leader. Small groups are one of the many contributors to spiritual growth. As members of small groups become Christ followers, the group becomes the family that helps them be in an environment that enables this transformational growth. People can have conversations with friends during this process, which aids to deepen relationships that enable transparency, a foundational principle for discipleship and transformational growth.

When Jesus said "Follow me", he gave an invitation that started a relationship for life change. The practice in this invitation for small groups is that God works to draw others as members share their stories with friends, neighbors, and co-workers. The opportunities for evangelism arise naturally through personal storytelling. Most of these stories happen in the context of life and in the community, which adds to the chance to share stories with the unchurched. One benefit to small groups is that many of them meet off the church campus during the week. While Bible study can happen anywhere, meeting in someone's home increases the opportunities to share life stories with people in the community.

A question is often asked, "Are groups that meet off the church campus better than groups that meet on campus?" Obviously, there is a difference these two environments for Bible study group experience. On campus groups have the benefits of not having to clean the house, childcare is usually more formalized and provided for by the church, and space is available for a group of any size. However, meeting on campus also contains hindrances, such as limited time to meet due to worship times or other groups using the space. There is also the limited knowledge of each other's family situations and children because of the formal meeting experience and members seldom see each other's family members. Another hindrance to meeting on campus for a small group is that most on-campus spaces are not designed for groups to eat together.

Meeting off campus brings with it an unlimited time to meet, although we recommend not meeting more than two hours per session. Off-campus groups can experience a leisurely meal together, which enables deeper conversation about life issues. By meeting in homes, each group member learns about the other member's lifestyles and interests. Since there is no technical time limit on the group's meeting, conversations can continue after the formal Bible study has ended. Through these post-meeting conversations among members, individual's lives become more transparent, and accountability starts. Whether you meet off campus or on campus, the key to reaching unconnected people is starting new groups. People like to try something new, and new small groups are often the best place to connect with new people. New groups can start anytime, in anyplace. These new groups increase the chances for evangelism and spiritual growth by increasing the opportunities people have to become involved.

Another aspect of small groups for evangelism is the community impact of events such as cookouts, Easter egg hunts, firework shows, and bonfires. In his book *The Search to Belong*, Joe Myers discusses the four spaces of community to which people spontaneously connect. These spaces are Public, Social, Personal and Intimate. The progressive nature of these spaces helps us to understand how Jesus' invitation to follow him leads to an intimate relationship of spiritual growth. Realizing these levels of spaces or relationships, described as soils in Matthew 13, can influence evangelism for groups. Jesus practiced the Public space concept in Matthew 14:13-21 when he fed five thousand people. Today, this might be a community event, such as an Easter egg hunt. Jesus also lived the Social space in Luke 10:1 when he sent out the seventy-two. Today, this might look like an intentional cookout with a few guests. The Personal space was where Jesus called the twelve disciples in Luke chapter 5. Personal space means the invitation becomes personal and introduces the opportunity to begin a new small group. The Intimate space is seen in Matthew 17:1 when Jesus sat with Peter, James, and John. This is an example of a discipling accountability group that can develop inside of the new small group. This accountability group begins after the regular Bible study time has ended, and the conversations after the meeting continue, most often in gender-based casual sub-groups.[67]

Jesus's invitation to follow him is only the first part of life as a Christ-follower. This is also a great starting place for small groups to begin their journey. The second phase brings with it the extended season of growth of which groups are a strategic part.

### Discipleship

After Jesus's invitation to follow him, he declares in the second part of this verse, "I will make you." Herein, the implications for discipleship are many. This phrase takes on the investment of time and intentionality of a journey with Jesus to grow. This growth takes place as a person spends time with Jesus and other Christ-followers. Spending time with Jesus includes Bible study, prayer, worshiping, serving, sharing, and other foundational practices of a disciple. It is by allowing these practices to become a way of life that will impact the individual and the people around them.

Discovering what has had the greatest godly impact on a person's or congregation's life can be very revealing and helpful for ministry planning. We found that life crises and mission trips were the top two discipling experiences in a person's life. Serving in an on-going ministry capacity was third. Small groups can give life to each of these opportunities. We cannot plan a crisis in a person's life, but we can be sure they are in a biblical community that can care for them during the crisis.

Mission trips offer an extended period in which a person can exclude the daily routines of life and focus on their relationship with Jesus as they serve him. Caution must be taken not to minimalize the life-changing impact of a mission trip with focus only on accomplishing the task for which the trip was intended. Knowing that life change can take place should raise planning mission trips to a high priority for church leaders. Small groups can participate as a team by going on a mission trip or supporting or collecting supplies for others to go. A simple goal for small groups, which could have a lifelong impact, could be for every group to send someone on a mission trip.

Serving ranked as the third highest rated practice that helps disciple people. A phrase that sums up the relationship between discipleship and serving is "The more you grow, the more you serve, and the more you serve the more you grow." Personal experience has shown that a person learns more about a subject and becomes more interested in a subject when they are asked to teach on that matter. Small groups help members volunteer to serve as they work together on a project, hold each other accountable to provide services in an ongoing ministry or to encourage serving by sharing the load of responsibilities in their small group.

Discipleship also happens as we build community through the study of God's Word and journey through life together. As mentioned earlier, many times the conversations before and after the regular Bible study times are when life change begins to take place. The accountability is part of these casual, personal discussions. Jesus has already made the promise to make us into his disciples. Small groups offer an environment that enables people to be receptive, to celebrate, and to multiply this transformation.

### Leader Development

The third phrase in Matthew 4:19 is "fishers of men." This phrase relates back to the Great Commission found in Matthew 28:19-20. The purpose for discipleship is not to gain more knowledge, but rather to fulfill the Great Commission. The phrase "fishers of men" implies intentionality towards reaching others and developing them into disciples. How can small groups be an intentional, challenging, and well-defined developmental process for discipleship and leadership? Matthew 4:19 shows the intentionality of Jesus's ministry by presenting the process from conversion to leadership in three short phrases. One great by-product of small groups is the built-in leader development. As the leader shares the load of leadership, he or she helps people to develop ownership and leadership experience. The story about my neighbor going from conversion to leadership exemplifies this principle.

Steve Gladen, the Small Groups Pastor of Saddleback Church, practices a plan for developing apprentices called "Crawl, Walk, Run."[68] This plan is a gradual process of leadership development that enables a leader to enlist a person to apprentice through a co-leadership journey. We adapted this process to fit our congregation by using the words "sentence, section, and study." "Sentence" involves giving the potential co-leader a sentence or question to lead at the next group meeting. This can be the icebreaker question or a key discussion question for the group. Once the new co-leader becomes more comfortable with speaking and guiding the group, he or she should be challenged to lead a section of the next study. Most Bible studies are broken down into sections, such as LifeWay's Bible Studies for Life curriculum, which uses a connect, explore, and transform outline.

Finally, the 'study' stage allows the co-leader to lead the entire meeting. Meet with the co-leader before the meeting for basic instruction on the role for the next meeting. Sometime after the small group meeting, take them to lunch and share positive, encouraging evaluation with them.[69] This graduated process makes it simple for a small group leader to develop potential leaders, not only for small group leadership but also for leadership in other areas of the church and life.

Matthew 4:19 also teaches another aspect of leader development in the phrase "I will make you." In Matthew 15:32-39, Jesus fed four thousand people, and, through this experience, he not only spoke to the thousands, but he also trained the disciples who had been with Jesus, watching, listening, and learning from their leader. Spending time together is an avenue to training.

Jesus did not leave the development of his disciples to large events only, however. He spent time with his twelve disciples. "After this, Jesus and his disciples went into the Judean countryside, where he spent time with them and baptized." (John 3:22 CSB). In Matthew 17:14-21, the disciples experienced a desire to learn more after they failed to heal a young boy. "Then the disciples approached Jesus privately and said, 'Why couldn't we drive it out?'" (Matt. 17:19 CSB). This was an opportunity for Jesus to teach them, but, for the disciples, it was a life-changing learning experience.

Small groups gain much of their success when people do life together through relationships. Staff and leaders should attempt to accomplish leadership development through this same model and through Jesus's example by spending time with leaders. Listening to and guiding other leaders is a valuable leadership tool. One of the most productive practices of leadership development is taking time to have coffee or lunch with small group leaders.

A few years ago, we were able to incorporate a motto into the small group's leadership development process called "Two minutes a day and pray on the way." This motto means to pray for a leader by name while on the way to work. Then, on the way home from work, call that leader to listen and share. These few minutes help to pass the time during the commute to work and help to personally customize any small group issues that may arise. It also gives ample time to show the concern for each leader. It is as simple as adding every leader's name and phone number to your contact list and using this process daily.

The development of volunteers into leaders is an ongoing journey. Though the example of the process from conversion to leadership found in Matthew 4:19 is clear, it is not easy. Leading transformational opportunities through small groups can cause lives to be changed, which in turn leads others to experience the same opportunities. This requires intentionality and obedience to the commands and promises of Jesus.

## CONCLUSION

Small groups are not only a place where evangelism and discipleship can occur, but they are also a place where people can be enabled and equipped to serve. Small groups can be the answer to more situations rather than just an avenue for Bible study as illustrated by my neighbor's story. Small groups are an avenue to caring for the congregation, developing leaders, and discovering more volunteers. One of the things often overlooked in small groups is the wealth of leadership development that is taking place on a week-by-week basis. I believe small groups are not only the best place for sustained life change to occur, but are also one of the most underrated and overlooked avenues for leader discovery and development.

Start where you are. Create a pilot small group season of six-weeks or three months with a group of close friends or potential leaders. Supply the pilot group with resources and studies that are designed to motivate people to multiply a group when finished, not just sign up for the next study. Record your discoveries and the God-stories each week and share them often with others. Clarify the goals and start new small groups as often as possible.

## Questions

1. How do you approach making a disciple?

2. What are the expectations of your small groups?

3. Is there a need in your community for more relationships among the people?

4. What would you consider success for your small group ministry?

5. Is there a clear path or scope and sequence for Bible study topics or curriculum in your small group?

6. Who was the last person you asked to "follow you?" This could be in the form of asking them join your group or be a disciple.

7. Ask yourself when is the last time you prayed for a person by name for their salvation?

# CHAPTER 6

# DISCIPLESHIP: DEPLOYED TO SERVE

## David Bond

"For even the Son of Man did not come to be served, but to serve…"

-Mark 10:45a (CSB)

In 1942, thirteen-year-old John Reed was hired as a busboy at the Davenport Hotel in Spokane, Washington. He initially made 35 cents an hour before moving up to the position of bellman and eventually head doorman. Wearing a 3-piece suit and top hat every day, Reed has greeted thousands of people over the years, including Presidents John F. Kennedy and George H.W. Bush. On June 1, 2017, the hotel honored Reed with a special pin for 75 years of service. The trophy company had to create a special pin for him because they had never seen someone with that length of tenure in one place! Some suggested that the company should make a 100-year pin because they did not expect John Reed to stop serving anytime soon.[70] Churches would love to have people so committed to service!

A connection between ministry service and discipleship is inescapable in Scripture. In Mark 3:13-19, Jesus called a group of followers among whom were the twelve apostles. Jesus stated in verse 14 that the Lord's two main purposes for these men were "to be with Him" and "to send them out to preach." "To be with Him" reflects the relational aspect of discipleship. Followers of Christ are to walk with Him, listen to Him, watch Him, and learn from Him. But discipleship is not only about spending time with Jesus. Discipleship is also about being "sent out" to actively demonstrate what has been heard from and seen in Christ. Jesus invested into the disciples relationally to prepare them for service.

Ephesians 4:12 outlines the role of the pastor as "equipping the saints for the work of ministry, to build up the body of Christ." Some leaders use this verse as a pastoral mandate for recruiting people to serve in the various volunteer roles necessary to carry out the programs of the church. However, further reading reveals that staffing volunteer positions is *not* the point of equipping saints for the work. Instead, the goal of equipping the saints for ministry service is to establish "unity in the faith and in the knowledge of God's Son, growing into maturity with a stature measured by Christ's fullness" (Eph. 4:13). The ultimate purpose of service is discipleship! Volunteers should not be encouraged to serve simply so that tasks will be accomplished, programs fully staffed, children well-cared for, and calendar obligations fulfilled. Rather, people in every church should be urged to find a place of ministry service because it is a necessary step on their journey to be fully developed followers of Jesus.

When church leaders equip saints for the work of the ministry and help them find a place to serve, they are doing much more than staffing a program or filling a position. Churches elevate ministry service because of its clear connection to true discipleship.

## SERVICE-DISCIPLESHIP MATTERS IN THE LOCAL CHURCH

Research reveals that when deploying people into service is viewed as discipleship, churches benefit in several important ways. First, discipleship and ministry service together decrease the likelihood that a person will leave one church to join another. One study in 2006 discovered that the top two reasons people gave for leaving a church were the lack of help in spiritual development and difficulty engaging in meaningful work at the church.[71] Service as discipleship encourages engagement for spiritual development.

Second, service-discipleship is a pathway to increasing the impact that a church is likely to have on its community. One large study of churches that had grown more than twenty percent or more over a five-year period revealed that more than nine out of ten members claimed involvement in ministry service, with a special focus on ministry outside the walls of the church.[72]

A third reason why service is an important emphasis for a church is its measurable impact on all other aspects of discipleship. Serving appears on a list of the eight attributes most closely connected to spiritual maturity as identified in the *Transformational Discipleship* study. Ed Stetzer reported that participants with high scores for the attribute labeled "Serving God and Others" also had higher scores for all other discipleship attributes. Stetzer's conclusion was that "growth leads to service and serving leads to growth – it's deeply connected."[73]

Finally, serving has an important educational value. The Great Commission calls us to make disciples by "teaching them to observe" all the commands of our Lord. Basic educational psychology speaks of three domains of learning: the mind (cognitive), the heart (affective), and the physical/behavioral (psychomotor). Our teaching engages the mind through Biblical content. Personal testimonies, videos, and life experiences connect mental concepts to our hearts and engage our emotions. But without opportunities to respond to truth through ministry service, our teaching fails to engage the behavioral domain and remains incomplete.

## SERVICE-DISCIPLESHIP AND THE BODY

In August 2016, heavy rain began to fall in southern Louisiana. When the storm finally passed, more than twenty-four inches of rain had fallen in a single day, causing devastating flood damage in Welsh, a town of 3,200 people. In the days that followed, First Baptist

Church began mobilizing people to respond with acts of service. The congregation, which averages around one hundred in attendance, fed over 70 disaster relief volunteers, helped clean the mud out of 52 homes and performed many other types of ministry service to hundreds of hurting people. In the months that followed, the church saw thirteen people make professions of faith in Christ and follow in baptism. The pastor remarked that the disaster provided an opportunity for the church to work more closely together than ever before and become more aware of the needs all around them.[74]

God used this opportunity for service to teach one congregation some important truths about the purpose of the church. But churches need not wait for disaster to strike before mobilizing the body for service. Consider the following lessons that Scripture teaches about the relationship of ministry service and the church:

1. *Service Illustrates the Intentional and Interdependent Design of the Body*

The human body is used as an illustration of the church for good reason. The body reflects a detailed design and maintains the distinctiveness of individual cells and systems while functioning together as a unified whole. 1 Corinthians 12:18 (CSB) states, "God has arranged each one of the parts of the body just as He wanted." The context tells us that these "parts" are individual persons who have each been given spiritual gifts, according to the will of God, to manifest the Holy Spirit and contributing to the common good of the body (v. 6-7). When disciples are encouraged to use their gifts, talents, and abilities to serve, they are giving testimony to God's intentional, unique design for their church.

A second way that the body is an illustration of the church is how each part depends on the others. The church is designed with each person depending on the gifts of another person to serve in ways that they themselves cannot. In this way, our service is designed to connect us to one another with the result of spiritual growth for the whole. 1 Corinthians 12:20-21 (CSB) instructs that no one part of the body can declare that it does not need the others. Instead, as Romans 12:5 (CSB) affirms, people are "individually members of one another." When all members of the church are using their gifts in ministry service, a healthy, interdependent body is the God-glorifying result.

### 2. *Service Provides Ways for Members to Build Up One Another*

Many people envision the discipling relationship as a one that is hierarchal between a more mature, experienced believer and a new follower of Christ. Service-discipleship utilizes "peer to peer" relationships to promote spiritual growth. Through service, any believer can be a part of building up the faith of another. Peter simplifies serving by teaching us that our gifts are a stewardship of the grace of God, given for serving others 1 Peter 4:10 (CSB). Paul teaches the church that one result of the work of the ministry is that the body of Christ is built up. (Ephesians 4:12 (CSB). No matter how long a person has been a believer or what his or her level of education or experience may be, service provides each person with a platform for building into the life of another.

### 3. *Service Contributes to a Healthy Church Environment*

The church environment described in the book of Acts depicts members serving one another in sacrificial ways. Acts 2 says that the fellowship of believers was "devoted" to the group, held "all things in common," met one another's needs, and "broke bread from house to house." These acts of service, combined with other discipleship practices such as the teaching of the word and prayer, contributed to an environment in which the Lord consistently added new converts. Again, the combination of cultivating a relationship with Jesus that results in outward acts of service provides a picture of biblical discipleship.

### 4. *Service is a Pathway to a Revitalized Church*

Most researchers indicate the number of declining churches ranges somewhere between 65 and 85 percent. While some will eventually die and/or be replanted, others have the chance to pursue revitalization. Mark Clifton shares that such churches must be committed to a more simplified strategy that includes "a lifestyle built around serving."[75] Serving the community is a non-negotiable part of revitalizing a ministry that has ceased to bear fruit.

Jesus provided a picture of the role of service in making a ministry fruitful again. In Luke 13:6-9, Jesus told of a fig tree that was found without fruit. Because the tree failed to bear fruit for three years, the vineyard owner instructed his worker to cut it down. But the vineyard worker asked for and received a reprieve for the tree, promising to dig and fertilize around it in hopes that fruit would appear once again. The picture is of hopeful renewal at the hands of a merciful master and a faithful worker. If declining churches are to be fruitful again, faithful servants must be willing to do the necessary works of service.

## SERVICE-DISCIPLESHIP AND THE LEADER

Eric Geiger has pointed out that Jesus continually discipled his followers relationally while simultaneously developing them as leaders.[76] In Jesus's ministry, two events provide a picture of service-discipleship from both the leader's perspective and from the servant's viewpoint. The feeding of the 5,000 is a good example of service-discipleship from the perspective of the leader. Found in all four gospels (Matthew 14:13-21, Mark 6:30-44, Luke 9:10-16 and John 6:1-13), this event provides at least five leadership principles for the pastor or ministry director to use when discipling people by connecting them to ministry service.

1. *Leaders Identify a Practical Need*

As was often the case, a large crowd had assembled to hear Jesus. But this time, the location was remote and the people needed to disperse to find an evening meal and a place to spend the night. Jesus knew this need and had compassion for the people.

Service-discipleship opportunities begin when leaders identify ministry needs around them. Mark Clifton wrote that learning how to "exegete the community" will reveal unique needs that could be met by ministry service.[77] Leaders cultivate compassionate hearts that look for local needs.

### 2. Leaders Have a Vision for a Ministry Response

When a need is identified, leaders must often encourage others to meet the need through ministry. The first response of the disciples was to send the people away so that they might find their own food and lodging. Already knowing what He was going to do, Jesus looked to His disciples and said, "You give them something to eat."

The natural tendency of the flesh is to seek self-interests and let someone else do the work of ministry service. Like Jesus, the leader looks into the eyes of the disciples and calls them to the work, knowing that it will lead them into a new and deeper encounter with God.

### 3. Leaders Utilize Present and Available Resources

Pastoral leadership has often been compared to coaching an athletic team. Jim Putman contrasts the approach taken by a college coach and a high school coach. A college coach scours the country to find players that someone else has developed and recruits them to join his team. A high school coach must take whatever players he has available and develop them into winners. For churches to win, leaders must develop their own players and use what they have.[78]

Mark's gospel records that Jesus instructed the disciples to "go and see" what was available. When the disciples found a boy with five loaves of barley bread and two fish, Matthew recorded Jesus saying simply, "bring them here to me." Jesus demonstrated that whatever they had would be sufficient to meet the need.

Leaders may be tempted to believe that if only more people, dollars, or facilities were available then more ministries could be accomplished. The model of Jesus is to assess present resources, use everything that is available, and entrust it to the Lord for maximum impact.

4.  *Leaders Empower People to Serve*

After Jesus blessed and multiplied the resources, he served the crowd by distributing the food through the disciples. Interestingly, Luke added that Jesus "kept giving" the bread and fish to the disciples as they set it before the crowd. Time after time, the disciples had a front row seat to watch what Jesus was doing, to follow His instructions, and to participate in the miracle that was taking place. Jesus fully intended this to be a transformational moment for His followers.

The acts of ministry that Jesus performed were not just to meet the immediate needs before them. Each act of ministry done in the presence of His disciples had an element of preparation and training along with it. In Luke's gospel, the feeding of the five thousand appears right after the disciples had returned from being sent out by Jesus to preach and to heal. Later, Luke recorded that seventy-two others were appointed and sent out in advance of Jesus' coming. In each case, Jesus intentionally involved, equipped, and sent out others to meet ministry needs. Their active service was an essential part of their growth.

5.  *Leaders Evaluate Ministry Impact*

One of the most often overlooked aspects of ministry service is the need to measure results. Good evaluation is necessary to make good decisions on future ministry methods. Lest evaluation seem unspiritual, all four gospel writers mentioned the same three measurements that took place among the crowd that day. First, a qualitative observation was made in that the people in the crowd were "satisfied." Everyone had as much as they wanted! Two other quantitative measurements were recorded in the five thousand men that were present and the twelve baskets of leftovers that remained. Someone was counting and evaluating the impact of this miracle!

Effective leaders are relentless about evaluation. Decide what type and level of impact would make the ministry a success, what measurements should be used to evaluate it, how reliable information can be obtained, and when the evaluation will take place. Jesus was not only meeting the need of five thousand men for a meal that day. He was continuing His practice of using ministry service as a tool for discipleship.

## SERVICE-DISCIPLESHIP AND THE SERVANT

One powerful picture of servanthood is more effective than any amount of skillful teaching. When I was in 10th grade, our youth group went on a mission trip to the inner city. We split into teams to accomplish several tasks at a mission center. One job was left unclaimed by any volunteer. At the back of the building was a dumpster overflowing with some of the vilest, repulsive garbage I had ever seen. The condition of the mess was such that the city refused to service it until the pile had been bagged and placed inside the container. This would require handling the garbage, placing it into bags, and making sure it could all fit inside the dumpster. Instead of sending me to do the work alone, our youth pastor volunteered to take on the worst job with me. As our leader, he modeled for all of us that no one is above even the most demeaning and disgusting work. His clear example of servant leadership left a lasting impression.

In John 13, Jesus provided the disciples with powerful teaching on what it means to be a servant. This time, He did not do so with a parable or a miracle, but with a demonstration. In an upper room, before Jesus shared His last Passover meal with the disciples, He washed their feet. In this act, He modeled for us the heart of the disciple for ministry service.

*Service is Motivated by Love*

John 13:1 says that what Jesus was about to do was a demonstration of his love for them. The connection of love and service stayed with John throughout his life. In 1 John 3:17-18 (CSB), the apostle wrote:

"If anyone has this world's goods and sees a fellow believer in need but withholds compassion from him – how does God's love reside in him? Little children, let us not love in word or speech, but in action and truth."

We have grown as disciples of Jesus when we are filled with the kind of love for others that motivates us to serve them. In many situations, the biggest challenge for ministry service is not a lack of hands, but of heart.

*Service Reflects Humility and Selflessness*

The image of Jesus with a towel tied around His waist and stooping to fulfill the servant's task of washing feet would have been unimaginably striking to the disciples. In Philippians 2, Paul implored the church to adopt the same selfless attitude of Jesus and "in humility consider others as more important than yourselves." Just as in the days of the early church, disciples today still struggle with the tendency to seek their own interests rather than humbly submit themselves in service to others.

*Service Allows Disciples to Meet Real Life Needs*

One of the reasons why Jesus washed the feet of the disciples was very practical: their feet were dirty! Because people traveled on dirt roads and mostly by foot, washing was necessary before reclining for a meal. Jesus demonstrated love and ministry service by meeting a practical need. In Acts 6, the disciples were confronted by another real need to care for the widows of the church and they responded by creating new opportunities for others to serve.

Today, many adults are being mobilized for ministry by meeting real-life needs. Some researchers have indicated that because of perceived consumerism in previous generations, young adults are especially drawn to organizations that provide opportunities to make an immediate difference through service. Some churches have even encouraged people to serve in some ministries as an entry point into the discipleship process, even prior to a profession of faith.[79]

*Service Creates Opportunities for Sharing Deeper Gospel Truth*

In John 13:6-11, the conversation between Jesus and Peter takes a turn into deeper theological waters. Jesus uses the practical ministry of washing feet to illustrate to Peter the bigger picture of what was about to take place through His atoning work on the cross.

Ministry service often provides opportunities for gospel conversations. Alvin Reid believes that people are more than twice as likely to allow a person to share their faith when evangelism is combined with simple acts of servanthood.[80] Service evangelism crosses cultures, generations, and contexts.

*Service Provides Visible Evidence of True Devotion to Christ (v. 12-17)*

Jesus concluded the lesson on servanthood by reminding the disciples of an important truth. If He, as Lord and Master, humbled Himself in ministry service, how much more should they be willing to do likewise? A heart that is willing to serve is evidence that Jesus is indeed Lord.

New believers often desire to show their gratitude to Jesus by finding a way to serve. In Luke 7, Jesus refused to turn away the woman who washed His feet with her hair and expensive perfume, noting that she did so because she had experienced great forgiveness. Today, those who experience life change as a forgiven disciple of Jesus should also desire to respond with service done in gratitude to Him.

Understanding the role of ministry service as a vital part of the discipleship process has a direct impact on church growth and health. The Bible is full of examples of how Jesus understood the need for serving both as a leader and as a servant Himself. Ministry is not only for a select few. Every Christian is called to minister – to fulfill his or her role in building up the body of Christ and reflecting the kingdom of God on this earth.[81] Ephesians 2:10 (CSB) says that we were "created in Christ Jesus for good works, which God prepared ahead of time for us to do." If you are saved, God has prepared work for you to do! Disciples are designed to be deployed into service.

## Questions

1. How do you begin to make disciples in your church?

2. When was the last time you prayed for a person by name for their salvation?

3. When was the last time you prayed for a person by name to serve in an area for which they are gifted, and not just the open position you need to fill?

4. Who was the last person you asked to "follow you"? This could be in the form of asking them to intern to join you in ministry or be a disciple?

5. How do you accomplish empowering of potential leaders?

6. Is there an intentional plan for leadership development?

7. Is the congregation aware of the program to develop leaders?

8. Is there a need in your community for more relationships?

9. What are the expectations of your small groups?

10. What is a success for the small group ministry?

11. Is there a clear path or scope and sequence for Bible study topics or curriculum?

## CHAPTER 7

# INTEGRATING DISCIPLESHIP AND MINISTRY LEADERSHIP IN YOUR PREACHING

## Adam Hughes

When you think of the public preaching of God's Word, what comes to mind? More specifically, what do you think it is about preaching or the goal of preaching that makes it important for the life of a local body? And, more precisely, what is the aim or goal of preaching in and for the local church? As a pastor, I know that during the times I did not approach my pulpit ministry purposely thinking through these questions and their answers, I found the impetus for and strategy of my preaching to be deficient and unintentional in producing spiritual results. Perhaps you are not like me. Perhaps you have never found yourself on this preaching carousel. If you have, however, I believe it is imperative that we ask ourselves a couple of questions. Does God's Word demand something more substantial of our preaching? Should we have a goal and strategic purpose for our platform ministry? I believe the answer to both questions is yes! In more than one place, the Bible affirms that we must have an intentional aim for our preaching.

A prime purpose of ministry leadership through preaching relates to the holistic spiritual formation of the individual believer and the body corporately. By this affirmation, I do not mean that preaching is the end of discipleship or the only means necessary to lead someone toward spiritual formation. I intend, however, to clearly convey that the platform ministry in our churches has a large role in the discipleship process. Jim Shaddix stated that "The process of disciple-making is most often initiated by preaching and is always carried along by it. And preaching bears its ultimate fruit in disciple-making as individuals grow to look more and more like Jesus."[82] If we are not intentionally understanding that preaching is a part of our ministry leadership that must be leveraged for spiritual formation, we are **not** using our pulpit ministry the way the Bible intends and commands us to. David Schrock stated "The Abiding truth remains: disciples are born by the preaching of the Word. So, we ask: What is the church making who has a complex system for 'discipleship,' but little emphasis on the Word of God? Discipleship does not end with gospel preaching, but it must begin with it."[83]

My goal in this chapter is to aid pastors in approaching their pulpit ministry as a catalyst for disciple-making in the church and to help them plan for it to do so. The premise of this chapter is that the pulpit is a key area of ministry leadership in the local church for discipling believers and that it must include the functions of evangelization of the lost and edification of the saint. The public preaching and teaching event in the local body is related intimately to the discipleship process of the church and the ministry leadership of the pastor. "While it's important for preachers to remember that disciple-making is more than preaching, it's equally important to remember that preaching is not less than disciple-making"[84], said Shaddix. Biblically, the pulpit then should integrate ministry leadership and discipleship. The public preaching and teaching ministry must begin with evangelism and move believers to growth and holistic spiritual formation.

In this chapter, I offer five practical guidelines for using your pulpit ministry as a catalyst for holistic spiritual formation in your church. These are practices I employed as part of my pulpit ministry that helped me to keep the goal of moving believers to growth and spiritual formation as a part of my public preaching ministry.

## USING THE PULPIT IN SPIRITUAL FORMATION

A significant text regarding the role of the pulpit as a catalyst for spiritual formation in the church is found in Acts 11. Acts 11:19-26, the narrative which introduces and describes the beginnings of the church in Antioch, concludes with the assertion that "the disciples were first called Christians at Antioch" Acts 11:26c CSB.[85] Notice, that as the context indicates and if our English translations are correct, "Christians" is not the term that the disciples gave to themselves. As a matter of fact, the term "Christian" is only used two other places in the New Testament – Acts 26:28 and 1 Peter 4:16. In all three locations, scholars have asserted that this was not a self-designated nor self-applied term. John Polhill explained, "In all three instances, it is a term used by outsiders to designate Christians. Evidently, the term was not used originally by Christians referring to themselves."[86] Also, the term "Christian" itself points to something significant about those holding the label. "The term (Christianoi) consists of the Greek word for Christ/Messiah (Christos) with the Latin ending ianus, meaning belonging to, identified by. . . . The term was often used by Roman writers to designate followers of Christ."[87], said Polhill. The disciples in the church at Antioch had become, to some degree, like Christ. The identification of "Christians" to the disciples in Antioch seems to indicate that the church in Antioch had become recognizable followers of Jesus and publically associated with Him. Therefore, if our goal is to leverage our preaching to help our people become more Christ-like, this passage seems to be a logical text to consider. I will use this narrative as a biblical foundation for the five guidelines below.

*First, recognize that your pulpit is a catalyst for discipleship and equipping the saints for holistic spiritual formation.* In Acts 11, we see clearly that a public teaching ministry contributed directly to the people's spiritual growth. Apparently, after seeing the scope of the movement of the Holy Spirit and magnitude of the task at hand in Antioch, Saul came to Barnabas's mind as one who could help with the discipleship ministry in the church. Therefore, Barnabas went and got Saul from Tarsus. Upon their arrival in Antioch, the predominant activity they engaged in for an entire year was teaching. "For a whole year they met with the church and taught large numbers. The disciples were first called Christians at Antioch" (Acts 11:26b). The text is primarily emphasizing the public preaching and teaching ministry in the church. At least two words in the text indicate as much. The word for "met" literally translates "to gather" or "bring together," and the word for "numbers" is the Greek word for "crowd". So, Saul and Barnabas were gathering the church and were teaching the crowd, not individuals, at this point in the life of the church in Antioch. I am sure that their teaching ministry included some one-on-one and small group sessions, as was a common practice of Jesus and Paul. However, this text is a prime biblical example of the truth that "the process of disciple-making is most often initiated by preaching and is always carried along by it. And preaching bears its ultimate fruit in disciple-making as individuals grow to look more and more like Jesus."[88]

As a pastor, I attempted to be mindful that every time I preached, I was influencing discipleship and disciple-making in my congregation. Ultimately, a pastor failing to impact and influence his people spiritually is impossible. The content of what we say and the way we preach relates directly to our people's spiritual maturity. "We want to see the members of our church grow in maturity. We want to see them learn to love God more, to love His Son Jesus more, to love one another more in Christ. We want them to be spiritually *alive*. That's what God's Word does when it is preached."[89] Even though our pulpit does not need to be the end of the discipleship process in our churches, it will either cause people to regress in their faith, allow them to stay where they are, or provide them with the sustenance and substance they must have to move forward in their journey toward Christlikeness.

In the pastorate, I found that simply approaching the pulpit on Sunday mornings with an awareness of its role in the discipleship process in the church made me more likely to have a positive impact on spiritual growth in my church. One way to be intentional about leveraging your pulpit for the spiritual formation and the disciple-making process of your people is to make sure that your messages' content is biblical, rich, and clear enough to be used for further discussion around the dinner table, the men's Tuesday morning discipleship small group, and any one-on-one mentoring relationships that are ongoing in your congregation. Mark Dever wrote, "That's because pastors teaching the Word is the core of a church's discipling ministry. It provides the food and water that feeds all the other discipling relationships within the church."[90] One practical way I facilitated this process in my church was to provide detailed notes and discussion guides from the pulpit. Occasionally, as the pastoral staff, we even provided some basic curriculum to accompany the Sunday morning messages. We found this practice to be helpful in facilitating and encouraging disciple-making conversations and relationship in the body.

These were some of the concrete practices I employed as a pastor to be intentional about discipleship in my public preaching ministry. Remember, the idea is to recognize that your pulpit does have a significant role in the spiritual formation of your people. The next two items in the list are essential for making your public preaching and teaching ministry a part of the holistic spiritual formation process in your church. As a local pastor, I exclusively held to the following practices in my preaching.

*Second, practice expository preaching generally.* This guideline and the next both deal with the content of what we should teach if we are going to produce a similar result that Saul and Barnabas produced from their public teaching ministry in Antioch. What was the content of Saul and Barnabas's pulpit? What were they "teaching?" Their content is at least implied in the description of the act of teaching. Biblically, we can gain a clue for the substance of their preaching and teaching in a couple of other significant passages on discipleship. First, in Acts 2:41-47, we see the daily operations of the infant church in Jerusalem. Many consider this to be a passage that describes the primary functions of the New Testament Church. We also are given some great insight into how the apostles were leading and discipling the early church. In verse 42, we read "They devoted themselves to the apostles' teaching . . . . (CSB)" The word "teaching" here is the noun form of the word "taught" from Acts 11:26. So, that Barnabas and Saul were teaching the Antiochian church that which constituted the "Apostles Doctrine" is likely. But, what is the "Apostles Doctrine?"

I believe we find the answer to this in Matthew 28, which lays out "The Great Commission." As one of the means for making disciples, Jesus instructed his disciples to teach "them to observe all that I commanded you" in verse 20. Again, the word "teaching" in Matthew 28:20 comes from the same root as the words in Acts 2 and Acts 11. Good evidence exists that Jesus' disciples taught the new church in Jerusalem what He Himself had taught them and commanded them to teach when making disciples. The "Apostles Doctrine," then, is most likely Jesus' teachings. The substances of Saul and Barnabas' public preaching and teaching ministry must have been what Christ taught His disciples to obey. Therefore, the content of our teaching must also be what Christ has taught us to obey in His Word. "At its core, discipling is teaching. We teach with words. We teach all the words that Jesus taught his disciples and all the words of the Bible."[91] Teaching what Christ has taught us to obey should work itself out in two ways in your pulpit. If your preaching ministry is going to serve as a catalyst for holistic spiritual formation in your church, then you must practice both general and systematic exposition.

General exposition relates to how I approached the content of any single sermon I ever preached. In other words, I understand that the depth of preaching is affected by general exposition. I believe basically only two broad ways to preach exist. We may either use the text to say what we want to say and emphasize what we want to emphasize, or we may allow the text to say what it wants to say and wants to emphasize. Many nuances of expository preaching exist and, perhaps many subcategories reside under the umbrella of expository preaching, but I believe expository preaching is essentially allowing the Bible to speak. "First, the nature of preaching as the heralding of God's Word means that all Christian preaching necessarily derives its authority from being rooted in and tethered tightly to God's Word, the Scriptures. Put more sharply, anything that is *not* rooted in and tethered tightly to God's Word is not preaching at all. It's just a speech."[92]

Therefore, I always strived to make sure that in each sermon I preached, I not only made points from my text but also made the points the text makes. A difference does exist between these two approaches. I attempted to emphasize in my sermon what the biblical author had chosen to emphasize, not some tertiary point or "embedded" doctrine. I held to, and continue to hold to, this practice whether preaching through a biblical book or a portion of a biblical book, a series leading up to Easter on the work of Jesus on the Cross, or an individual message on the roles of men and women in marriage from Ephesians 5. I believe that general expository preaching has several benefits for the holistic spiritual formation of your people and must be practiced for your public preaching and teaching ministry to be useful in disciple-making for several reasons. Perhaps the most significant reason is that God's Word, content, and truth is going to change lives and grow believers, not your content or my content. "Because you have been born again-- not of perishable seed but of imperishable-- through the living and enduring word of God. . . . like newborn infants, desire the pure milk of the word, so that you may grow up into your salvation, if you have tasted that the Lord is good" (1 Peter 1:23; 2:2-3, CSB). Therefore, strive to make sure that the content of every sermon is God's intended content. As Shaddix stated,

> The most effective and direct way to foster spiritual growth in your people is to lay open the supernatural text, called the Scriptures, in such a way that the Holy Spirit's intended meaning and attending power are brought to bear on their lives. Expository preaching unleashes the full transformation and re-creative power of God's truth. It enhances biblical literacy by explaining the truth in context and allowing Scripture to interpret Scripture. It develops people's appetite for God's Word and encourages them to go home and search the Scriptures for themselves. And expository preaching models for your people how they should study the Bible and interpret it with integrity. If you

want to see your flock grow spiritually, expose them to God's truth on a regular basis.[93]

*Third, rely on systematic exposition specifically.* If general exposition deals with the depth of preaching and the content of an individual sermon, then systematic exposition covers the breadth of preaching and has an eye toward the content of your entire preaching ministry. By systematic exposition, I mean the decision to and practice of preaching consecutively through biblical books or significant portions of a biblical book in a series of sermons. My regular practice as a pastor, frankly over 90% of my preaching, encompassed this type of preaching. "At its core, discipling is teaching. We teach with words. We teach all the words that Jesus taught his disciples and all the words of the Bible. Corporately, this is why my own church preaches expositionally and *consecutively* through books of the Bible . . . ."[94] I believe this method and philosophy of preaching is the best way to use your public preaching and teaching ministry to foster discipleship and disciple-making in your church. Greg Ogden wrote, "It is particularly important in our day that a disciple has the opportunity to cover the essential teachings of the Christian life in a systematic and sequential fashion as a means of cultivating this new reality."[95]

There are many reasons why this method of preaching is helpful for holistic spiritual formation in your church. First, it systematically exposes your people to larger portions of the corpus of Scripture. It causes us as both preachers and congregants to deal with passages of Scripture that we usually do not. Second, it fosters a greater appreciation of God's Word in the way He delivered it to us. It encourages your congregation to read the Bible for themselves, and it patterns for them how to interpret Scripture rightly in context. Third, it provides solid biblical curriculum for the disciple-making relationships and conversations that hopefully are occurring in your church.

Finally, it is the method of preaching that best matches Jesus' words in the Great Commission to teach those we are discipling "to obey everything He has commanded us . . . .". Francis Chan explained,

"As we have said, an important part of making disciples is teaching people to obey everything Jesus commanded (Matt. 28:20). This means that we need to know Jesus's teaching and commands. It may seem that the first disciples had an advantage on us here. How can we teach people to follow Jesus if we haven't observed His ministry and listened to His teaching? But we are not at a disadvantage at all because God has recorded His words and the testimony of Jesus's followers in a book – the Bible."[96]

*Fourth, allow an evangelistic mindset to drive your use of application.* Two realities drove this guideline in my ministry. The first one is obvious whereas the second may be less recognized and acknowledged. First, if people do not come to faith in the Lord Jesus Christ and are not redeemed in our churches, then we do not have anyone to disciple and see grow toward Christlikeness in the church. Second, if your church is anything like the ones I pastored, then more than likely you have unredeemed people sitting under your preaching every week, including people who are on your rolls as members. Due to these two facts, I understood as a pastor that evangelism and evangelistic preaching were paramount and an imperative in my life and pulpit. "One of the most important things we do when we stand to preach is *herald the good news of Jesus Christ*. We make Christ known, and we make known the good news that salvation is to be found in Him. . . . We should preach to evangelize."[97]

Notice in Acts 11, evangelism was a large part of the initial and ongoing public preaching and teaching ministry of the church. Extravagant and impartial evangelism was characteristic of the ministry in Antioch. "But there were some of them, men from Cyprus and Cyrene, who came to Antioch and *began* speaking to the Greeks also, proclaiming the good news about the Lord Jesus" (Acts 11:20, CSB). Now, to be sure, these men shared the gospel in their private one-on-one conversations, but if the pattern of Acts holds true, we must interpret this verse to mean that their practice of evangelism also occurred among the crowds as a part of a public preaching ministry as well. Not only this, implied later in the text is that this emphasis on evangelism continued in church even while disciple-making was being enacted and celebrated. "When he [Barnabas] arrived and saw the grace of God, he was glad and encouraged all of them to remain true to the Lord with devoted hearts, for he was a good man, and full of the Holy Spirit and of faith. And large numbers of people were added to the Lord" (Acts 11:23-24, CSB). Again, I believe good evidence exists to understand this characteristic as a part of both their private conversations and their public "pulpit."

The primary way I applied this in my pulpit was to make a direct and specific application every week. Knowing that a significant portion of the Bible, and most of the New Testament, was originally addressed to believers does not mean that every passage fails to hold an application for the lost that can and should be communicated. For several reasons, most of which we do not have the space to explore here, I believe one and only one application exists for all unbelievers in every text of Scripture – repent and believe on the Lord Jesus and be saved! A primary reason for my position is because someone who is unregenerate and therefore without the Holy Spirit is incapable of fully participating in the activities and the lifestyle to which the Word of God calls and commands believers.

Therefore, even though not every passage of Scripture is an evangelistic text, this does not mean that we cannot and should not make evangelistic appeals in every expository sermon. In fact, I believe we must! So from my pulpit, regardless of whether I was preaching on having a gospel-centered marriage from Ephesians 5, the call to live a God-glorifying life in light of the Kings reign in the heart of a believer from the Sermon on the Mount, or the command to live a life free from the bondage of sin from Romans 6, I explicitly and consistently made one application to the lost in every sermon: "This passage is a call for the believer to come and obey in light of his redemption and in the power of the Gospel. However, if you are an unbeliever you are incapable of obeying God's Word fully in this way. Therefore, this passage is a call for you to repent and believe on the Lord Jesus and live!" Dever and Gilbert wrote,

> "In everything – from the way we introduce our sermons, to the way we illustrate our points, to the way we bring everything down to the conclusion – we preach with the goal of spurring believers on in their maturity in Christ and of awakening nonbelievers to their need for the Savior. In a word, that answers that we preach with two main aims, to *edify* and to *evangelize*."[98]

*Finally, understand that your public preaching is a major part of your leadership, whether intentional or unintentional.* Aubrey Malphurs gives us a definition of Christian Leadership in the following statement: "Christian leadership is the process whereby servants use their credibility and capability to influence people in a particular context to pursue their God-given direction."[99] Is there any evidence that Saul and Barnabas's pulpit influenced the people of the church at Antioch to pursue their God-given direction? Yes, in at least two ways. In Acts 13, a passage which chronicles the beginning of the missionary movement from the Antioch church, we have biblical validation for the role the pulpit holds in pastoral leadership. Barnabas and Saul's public teaching and preaching ministry seem to have been a part of the leadership development process in the church that led others to take responsibility for the congregation. Now, instead of having only two teachers, the church appears to have an additional three individuals who hold some office and responsibility. "Now in the church at Antioch there were prophets and teachers: Barnabas, Simeon who was called Niger, and Lucius of Cyrene, Manaen, a close friend of Herod the tetrarch, and Saul" (Acts 13:1, CSB).

Furthermore, through their pulpit, Barnabas and Saul also must have influenced the Antiochian believers toward a corporate adoption of God's vision from the Great Commission. It is from this local church, not from the one in Jerusalem as we might expect, that the first intentional and organized missionary enterprise began. "'Set apart for Me Barnabas and Saul for the work to which I have called them.' Then after they had fasted, prayed, and laid their hands on them, they sent them off" (Acts 13:2b-3, CSB). Even though the two primary leaders ultimately are the ones who go and carry the weight of the mission, Acts leaves no doubt that the mission itself resulted from corporate obedience and that Saul and Barnabas understood their roles were set within and accountable to a corporate initiative. One place this becomes clear is at the end of Acts 14. Upon their return from the mission field, God's Word says, "From there they sailed to Antioch where they had been commended to the grace of God for the work they had now completed. After they arrived and gathered the church together, they reported everything God had done with them and that he had opened the door of faith to the Gentiles" (Acts. 14:26-27, CSB).

Clearly, a part of the impact of Saul and Barnabas's preaching and teaching ministry was their ministry leadership and leadership development within the church. From their pulpit, they moved individuals and the body corporately toward their God-given direction. Your preaching and teaching ministry can and should have a similar influence among your congregation.

Bruce Bickel in his book *Light and Heat* has given a philosophy of ministry leadership through the example of the Puritan model, which was related to their public preaching ministry. He explained the effect the Puritan philosophy should have on our churches now: "Sensing the Puritan preacher's commitment to his pastoral ministry as an extension of the pulpit ministry gives excitement in comprehending what properly equipped leaders could do in a local church. Leadership development must be a priority for every pastor."[100] We should appreciate the emphasis such a philosophy places on the personal development of our people and how it moves them to their God-given direction. As a preaching practitioner, I believed leadership development was "a must" for my pulpit.

Understanding the role that my public preaching and teaching ministry held in the spiritual formation of my congregation, I found that I was more effective in integrating my ministry leadership and discipleship through the pulpit if I approached leading with some intentionality. The question is not will you lead from the pulpit. The question is will you lead well and take your people to their God-given direction from your pulpit. Your people will understand what you value by what you say from the pulpit. Your people will know what you want and expect of their lives by the level of specificity of your application. Your people will know what you believe the mission of the church to be by the content of the text that you preach and the points you allow God to drive home from your pulpit. My practical encouragement to you would be to be intentional with the values you communicate from the pulpit, make specific applications in your messages that call people to develop into Christlikeness and servants in the church, and preach often on books and passages of Scripture that remind your congregation of the Gospel and our Gospel mission. James White wrote,

> "The purpose of the church is such an important item to keep before the church that many preachers include an annual series on the mission of the church in their sermon planning. Whether its form takes shape as four sermons on the four tasks of the church (worship, ministry, evangelism, and discipleship) or as an exposition of the book of Acts in light of the mission of the early church, such a series serves as an annual reminder that everything the church engages itself in relates to the mission of the church."[101]

## THE CASE OF TRANSFORMING TOM

As a pastor, I have observed the role that preaching plays in both initiating the disciple-making process and carrying it along in individuals' Christian experiences many times over. One man, in particular, comes to mind. Tom was a city bus driver. He had been married several times and had one adult daughter. He had recently become a new grandfather. Before I met him, Tom had attended church on a somewhat regular basis. He did so more out of compulsion and a belief that to not do so would anger God more than any other reason. However, he had never made a public profession of faith, been baptized, or become an official member of a church. The first conversation I had with Tom was in a local Starbucks over a cup of coffee. I shared the Gospel with him, which he said he believed, but he responded, to my dismay, not with surrender but by questioning his need to surrender to Christ because he had "always believed that."

The next Sunday, however, Tom was in church with his daughter. As a matter of fact, for the next two years, other than when he was out of town, he did not miss a Sunday. He endured my lengthy sermon and listened attentively as I feebly attempted to expound some section of Acts. Then, when I opened the invitation and gave instructions for how to respond to the Gospel, Tom and his daughter both publically came forward. Later in a counseling room, they both prayed to receive Christ. On Father's Day, I had the privilege of baptizing them both. This story would be amazing if it ended there, but his surrender to Christ was only the beginning for Tom, our relationship, and his process of growing into Christlikeness. I began to meet with Tom weekly. I was blessed to witness a spiritual transformation. Tom was transformed from a man who did not understand the Gospel to one who desired the Gospel to drive his daily life, a man who had been married multiple times to one who wanted Christ to be Lord of all his relationships, and a man who had never been committed to a local church to one who became so committed that he would call and ask me for my sermon text on the rare occasion he had to miss a Sunday morning so that he could "keep up."

Most of the discussions at our meetings and the content of his discipleship grew out of the content of my expository sermons. In the beginning, I was not the one who initiated this practice. Tom did. I would arrive with an agenda or a discipleship curriculum to cover. Tom, however, always had questions concerning my sermon from the previous Sunday. After dealing with these items, we rarely had time to get to what I had planned. I was beginning to get frustrated, but then

I noticed something unique happening. As I answered his questions and we discussed the sermon, the Holy Spirit began to grow Tom and form him into the likeness of Christ. Before long, although perhaps not in an official capacity, Tom became a leader in our church. He was taking the initiative to serve the body when an opportunity arose, invite people to church, and introduce lost people to Jesus.

## CONCLUSION

This process in Tom's life was an application of Acts 11 and a practical outworking of these five guidelines in real life. His discipleship process did not end with the preaching of the Word, but it began there. Pastors, most who enter the journey toward Christlikeness will begin under the preaching of some pastor, perhaps yours. So, practically, it is accurate to say that the discipleship process does not end with the preaching of the Word, but it most often begins there, as Shaddix described.

> "Most often the disciple-making process begins when the Word of God is preached to the crowd. Something mysterious takes place there. As the Scriptures are expounded, people are convicted about sin and complacency (see Neh. 8:1-12). Their hearts burn within them as did the hearts of the two disciples on the Emmaus road (see Luke 24:27, 32). As the Word is read, explained, and applied, people are compelled to greater holiness (see 1 Tim. 4:13-16). They are convinced that something otherworldly is taking place, and they are constrained to yield their lives a bit more to the things of God."[102]

Your public preaching and teaching ministry will affect discipleship and the disciple-making process in your church at some level. My prayer is that this chapter and these five guidelines will help you be more prepared and intentional with those who are on this journey under your care.

## CHAPTER 8

# INTEGRATING DISCIPLESHIP AND MINISTRY LEADERSHIP: A BIBLICAL AND PHILOSOPHICAL FOUNDATION

## Randy Stone

## A PERSONAL PHILOSOPHY FOR MINISTRY LEADERSHIP

Christmas Day 1776 is indelibly marked in American history. Perhaps you've seen the infamous painting of General George Washington crossing the Delaware into the Battle of Trenton. Managing meager supplies and fighting a bitter winter, the Commander-in-Chief won a crucial battle over the Hessians encamped there. While the victory was important, the following ten days proved to be more so. Washington coordinated a surprise attack on the British forces in Princeton by first commissioning 500 men to maintain camp and campfires. By muffling the wagon wheels and extinguishing the torches, he marched the remaining 4,500 troops twelve miles throughout the night and surrounded the British army under the command of Cornwallis. The stealthy approach allowed the modest and outnumbered army to cut off Cornwallis's support from other British reinforcements. These two victories inspired and united the nascent Continental Army and solidified Washington's reputation as a military mastermind. His fierce determination, military savvy, and decisive leadership were crucial to ultimate triumph in the Revolutionary War and the eventual establishment of a new country.[103]

Effective leadership was and continues to be crucial to the survival and success of our republic. Effective leadership is vital for the contemporary church as well. Churches today are in need of more decisive leaders with a similar determination with the emphasis on spiritual savvy rather than military savvy. Digital and literary landscapes are bursting with resources on leadership. Leadership consultants and coaches appear to be everywhere. Nevertheless, many churches languish from a leadership vacuum. This chapter will present a biblical and theological foundation of leadership accompanied by a framework for equipping church leaders.

Four aspects of a personal philosophy of ministry leadership will be presented in this chapter, which are as follows: Commission, Calling, Character, and Competency. Each aspect directly influences the capacity for successful endeavors within the Kingdom of God. The Commission or divine purpose derived directly from God and his eternal work, is non-negotiable. The Callings on his people and ministers are irrevocable. Creator God bestows on each person Character and Competencies, distinct qualities and capabilities which can either elevate or limit potential. These four aspects determine the ultimate impact of leaders in their spheres of influence.

## COMMISSION

In the iconic scene from the classic film Lord of the Rings, an argument over the fate of the indestructible ring exemplifies inherit distrust among those who coveted its possession. An unlikely hobbit hero assumes the dangerous task of returning the ring to its place of origin, thereby ridding the world of the ring's chaos. Yet the hobbit

Frodo could not have completed his mission without a team. Each member of the team came from a different background and culture, possessing different skills and abilities. The "fellowship of the ring" was forged by each member's pledge to fulfill the mission. Together they overcame differences and vowed to accomplish a greater shared goal.[104]

The greater shared goal of the church is joining God in his kingdom work. The mission spans all of human history, from the creation of the first man to the crucifixion of the first Son to the coronation of the final King. Manifested by the Father, Jesus and Spirit, God sought relationship and reconciliation with His creation. Leaders who separate their efforts and energies from this divine quest exert themselves in vain. Effective leaders must have a clear understanding of God's desire and paramount aim as he relates to humankind and the church.

God created man in his image and breathed life into him.[105] The first man, Adam, was placed in the garden and given one task and one prohibition. The sole task was to care for creation; the one prohibition was to avoid the fruit of a single tree, the tree of the knowledge of Good and Evil.[106] Man, of course, failed to keep this one prohibition and was therefore banished from the garden, unable to fulfill his only task.

God's fellowship with Adam and Eve is evident from the opening chapters of Genesis. God seemed to walk and communicate with the first couple until the relationships were severed by sin. God's intention to seek and restore this broken relationship is revealed in Genesis 3:9 when he asks "Where are you?" to Adam and Eve. From that moment on, his actions demonstrate his desire to make the relationship with his creation and especially humankind new again.

Generation after generation, God sought to reconcile his fallen creation to himself. Jesus injected himself into human history with an act of love predetermined before creation and the beginning of time.[107] Jesus, who is God, became a man. He was miraculously conceived, born in relative obscurity, and then raised in the shadows until he launched his public ministry.

Jesus was single-minded about his purpose. Jesus' life was marked by total surrender to fulfill the mission assigned to him by the Father, demonstrated by his every word and action.[108] He willingly sacrificed his own life as a substitution for ours.[109] On the eve of his death, Jesus' prayer expresses his sense of mission, "This is eternal life, that they may know You, the only true God, and Jesus Christ whom You have sent. I glorified You on the earth, having accomplished the work which You have given Me to do."[110] **Jesus declared "Mission Accomplished!"** However, he left his followers and the church with a final mission to make disciples by reaching and restoring the lost into a relationship with God.

The Great Commission clearly extends to the early church. In 2 Corinthians 5:11-21, now one of my favorite passages, I discovered four important elements in God's restoration project, the ministry of reconciliation:

- Motivation: Love is the motivation for seeking to restore the lost.

- Message: Christ died and rose on behalf of those who were separated from him.

- Method: We persuade, model, beg and proclaim the message.

- Manifestation: The evidence of effective ministry is changed lives.

I live on the New Orleans Baptist Theological Seminary campus in the city. We are surrounded by deep poverty, excessive crime, and cultural diversity. I often feel as if I am in a foreign country. This passage reminds us that we are God's ambassadors, representing Him and His Kingdom in the foreign land called Earth. The mission is not yet complete. Our task is not over. We must press on toward the work God has given us to do.

# CHARACTER

*The key to successful leadership today is influence, not authority.*

- Ken Blanchard, Author Speaker,
Leadership Consultant

Now let us turn our attention to the character of leaders called by God. Henry Blackaby warned that "Some have resorted to developing the appearance of a leader rather than developing the character of a leader."[111] I will present three important qualities vital for leadership success and two guardrails important for leadership longevity.

God has used numerous individuals, all of them flawed, to lead his people. Abram was a liar, Moses was a murderer, David was an adulterer, Gideon was a doubter, Samson was a womanizer, Samuel was an inadequate parent, and the list goes on. Yet despite their personal failures, their names are recorded in scripture for all eternity. Therefore, rather than focusing on human weaknesses, let us highlight three characteristics associated with biblical leaders who are worthy of honor and emulation: humility faith, and courage.

*Humility*

In our self-centered American culture, the word humility is seldom uttered and even more seldom exemplified. Yet, humility is central to biblical leadership. Imagine the challenges Moses faced, leading a group of people to a place he had never been. He faced uncertain opposition establishing a new social, religious and cultural center. Moses' followers were hundreds of thousands of slaves who had been accustomed to oppressive taskmasters for generations. It is hard to be critical of leadership under those circumstances.

Moses could have been proud of growing up in Pharaoh's home, for escaping the hardships of slavery, and for having such a personal connection with God, but he was not. In fact, the opposite was true, as is described in Numbers 12:3 (CSB), "Moses was a very humble man, more so than anyone on the face of the earth."[112] Wow. Would God say that of you and me?

Humble leaders permeate the biblical story. God chose leaders from among the lowly and unassuming and exalted them to positions of authority and influence. In Psalm 149, the anonymous psalmist reminded the readers and seekers of God, "For the Lord takes pleasure in his people, he adorns the humble with salvation."[113] Daniel, David, and Epaphroditus are just a few examples of whom humility was a defining characteristic for each one.

Jesus' life exemplified humility. He was born to an unwed mother, the son of an uncertain Father, and did not even have a bed. At his death, he hung between two thieves, enduring the ridicule and scorn of an ignorant and unbelieving mob. Paul writes in Philippians, "And being found in appearance as a man, he humbled himself by becoming obedient to death—even death on a cross!"[114] Humility was not only Jesus' example, but it was also his expectation. To his disciples and followers, he declared that humility must precede greatness and prominence. [115] He masterfully and lovingly demonstrated by washing his disciples' feet.

*Faith*

A second defining quality of biblical leaders is faith. Justification comes by faith. Faith is the way of salvation and the source of righteousness.[116] Actions taken apart from faith are a sin.[117] Beyond the aspect of personal salvation and right standing before God, a vital faith life is essential for the leader. Can we believe God for an unseen future? Can we wait on God when his provision is not yet in sight?

Faith or the lack thereof, is a central point in Jesus' teaching. Throughout the gospels, Jesus commended faith while he condemned a lack of faith. He acknowledged faith-filled individuals like the widow who gave her last two coins, yet Jesus admonished his faithless wave-tossed disciples in the midst of a stormy sea.

The early church movement is marked by men and women of faith who believed and trusted God for their very existence and success. The writer of Hebrews defined faith as "the substance of things hoped for"[118] and instructed readers that "without faith it is impossible to please God."[119] Effective and honorable leaders in the Bible demonstrated enduring faith and relentless obedience.

*Courage*

Since the fall of man, God's people have faced severe adversity and persecution. God-called leaders must exhibit courage in the face of challenges inside and outside the church. When Joshua assumed the mantle of leadership from Moses, he faced "giants in the land," ignorance among the assembly, and inexperience among the elders. Only a handful of people survived the forty years of testing. God repeated to Joshua the same words he spoke to Moses: "Above all, be strong and very courageous to observe carefully the whole instruction my servant Moses commanded you. Do not turn from it to the right or the left, so that you will have success wherever you go." (Joshua 1:7; 2 Chron. 32:7; Deut. 31;6 CSB). Similar exhortations are recorded elsewhere in Scripture as God called out faithful leaders to face their enemies.

In the New Testament, Jesus trained and prepared followers for Kingdom living and leading. The twelve disciples were more than religious zealots of a new sect; they were the first recruits of a new spiritual army from a heavenly Kingdom. Obviously, the disciples misunderstood the task before them. A common refrain spoken by Jesus to build up their faith and courage was, "Take courage! It is I. Don't be afraid." (Mark 6:50b, CSB)

Exponential church growth and expansion pressured existing religious, social, and political systems of the first century, which in turn forced authorities toward the persecution of Christians. In light of these realities, Paul admonished the saints at Corinth, "Be alert, stand firm in the faith, be courageous, be strong."(1 Cor. 16:13, CSB). Sound familiar? With the upheaval in religious, social and political systems, leaders today need a renewed call to be strong and courageous.

*Conduct Guardrails*

Leaders are more likely to lose their positions and reputations from a moral, ethical or relational issue than an incompetent ministry. How is one leader seemingly insulated from issues while another is plagued with problems? Conscience and spiritual standards serve as guardrails in our endeavors to live a God-honoring life.

God instilled an intrinsic moral compass, "a conscience", in each person. Paul and Peter both refer to the role of the conscience to guide our choices. Paul explicitly declared, "I always strive to have a clear conscience toward God and men" (Acts 24:16, CSB). Peter affirmed that sentiment with,

> "But in your hearts regard Christ the Lord as holy, ready at any time to give a defense to anyone who asks you for a reason for the hope that is in you. Yet do this with gentleness and respect, keeping a clear conscience, so that when you are accused, those who disparage your good conduct in Christ will be put to shame. For it is better to suffer for doing good, if that should be God's will, than for doing evil." (1 Peter 3:15-17, CSB).

A leader must be disciplined to tirelessly pursue a clear conscience. Likewise, leaders must examine and establish spiritual standards for themselves and their organizations. Determining applicable spiritual standards can be tenuous. Some inappropriate social morals or practices are explicit in Scripture while others seem to be contextualized. A plethora of behaviors falls into this category, including the following three prevalent principles:

1. When certain behaviors are clearly communicated in the Bible, make them part of your lifestyle.

2. Behaviors which appear to be "gray" in the Bible should be tested. If and when you engage in a certain behavior, do you feel a conviction from the Holy Spirit? Does this behavior offend other believers and more importantly unbelievers?

3. Does the behavior in question exalt God and build up the body of Christ? Is the behavior beneficial for your personal health or emotional well-being? (1 Cor. 6:12, 10:23).

In his book *Redefining Leadership*, Joseph Stowell juxtaposed character-driven leadership with outcome-driven leadership and questions current measurements of success. He asked the penetrating question, "What if there is more at the core of successful leadership, particularly for spiritual leaders than the mere accomplishment of organizational goals, the growth of the enterprise, and the name recognition of the leader?"[120] I submit that character must be a part of the true measure of success.

## CALLING

*The ministry is a terrible vocation but a wonderful calling.*
Jimmy Draper, Former President, Southern Baptist
Convention and Lifeway Resources

If you are looking for a good career, path ministry is probably not it. If you feel called to ministry, you must answer. Christian leaders respond to two callings in their lives: individual and congregational. The individual call is one of obediently following Christ. The congregational call is concerned with ministry function and role within the church. As Blackaby stated, "Calling comes before vocation."[121]

Before we can lead, we must be willing to follow. Jesus called the first disciples with these words, "Follow me!"(Matt. 16:24). The initial call is to walk away from self-centeredness toward Christlikeness, the ultimate goal of our obedience. Following Christ does not call for a causal relationship but rather a zealous obedience. As noted previously, the aim of the Great Commission is not just information but sincere obedience. Christ followers who have never learned obedience to the Word and promptings of the Holy Spirit will never be equipped to lead others. Obedience is more than a spiritual practice; it is a lifestyle to embrace and experience.

The second calling is to tend the congregation. Only a few New Testament passages identify or label leaders. Leaders are not to impose their positions or authority but instead are to serve and support the people of God. Additionally, leaders bear responsibility for the care of the people and will be held to greater account by God.

Defining a call to a specific ministry leadership role is the obvious next consideration. All organizations need different leaders with different callings and gifts to accomplish the goals of the organization. The church is no different. Churches are led by staff members who have a variety of calls. A combination of functional leaders allows the church to fulfill the mission of making disciples.

New Testament leadership organizational models appear in contrast to Old Testament examples. New Testament roles and assignments are more parallel than they are hierarchical, as in the Old Testament. Missionaries appointed elders, the predominant congregational decision makers, to protect and care for local gatherings of believers.

Perhaps no passage of scripture explains more fully the relationship between church leadership and individual spiritual development than Ephesians chapter four. Five leadership positions for the church are acknowledged in this text: apostles, prophets, evangelists, pastors, and teachers. Each position is important to equip the saints for the work of ministry. Churches need some or all of these roles activated to fully prepare the members of that body. Paul wrote in Ephesians 4:11-17 (CSB),

"And he himself gave some to be apostles, some prophets, some evangelists, some pastors and teachers, equipping the saints for the work of ministry, to build up the body of Christ, until we all reach unity in the faith, and in the knowledge of God's Son, growing into maturity with a stature measured by Christ's fullness. Then we will no longer be little children, tossed by the waves and blown around by every wind of teaching, by human cunning with cleverness in the techniques of deceit. But speaking the truth in love, let us grow in every way into him who is the head—Christ. From him the whole body, fitted and knit together by every supporting ligament, promotes the growth of the body for building up itself in love by the proper working of each individual part. Therefore, I say this and testify in the Lord: You should no longer live as the Gentiles live, in the futility of their thoughts."

I began my ministry as a Christian educator believing that "if people knew right, they would do right." Unfortunately, I was wrong. Through interactions with thousands of people, I have discovered that the key to spiritual growth is ministry engagement. As people "do right," they increasingly "know and grow right." The obvious principle to extract is that equipped and serving saints grow in three areas: unity, knowledge and spiritual maturity. All of which are desirable outcomes in any ministry context.

Let me explain how this spiritual growth spiral works. A new believer or nominal church attendee begins serving. First, he or she must trust God and rely on the Holy Spirit which produces maturity. Uncertainty and unfamiliarity with tasks motivate a person to seek information from the Bible or others experienced in ministry, resulting in knowledge. In most instances, effort based on knowledge and fueled by faith yields spiritual maturity and ministry success. Consequently, the reward for ministry success is greater responsibility, a principle supported by the teachings of Christ as recorded in Luke 19:11-27. Then, the spiral begins again. The servant assumes a new task, trusts God, relies on the Holy Spirit, seeks knowledge to accomplish the task, and God grants success. The spiral continues as a person grows in these three areas of unity, knowledge and spiritual maturity.

Finally, in my experience, church members who are engaged in meaningful ministry, sensing empowerment of the Spirit, and growing in faith and knowledge are less likely to cause division in the church. They are often oblivious to internal conflicts or, if aware, seek to become peacemakers within the body. On the other hand, members with no meaningful place of ministry contribute to conflict or sow seeds of discord. Mobilized members serving in meaningful ministry is "proper working" and causes "growth of the body."

Applying a philosophy, strategy, and structure for church organization is vitally important. The integration of leadership and discipleship cannot be understated.

## COMPETENCIES

*If your actions inspire others to dream more, learn more, do more, and become more, you are a leader.*

- John Quincy Adams

Scripture reinforces the uniqueness of each individual and God's intention for each person to engage in "good works" for his glory. (Eph. 2:10). We realize our full potential by discovering and developing personal and general competencies.

### Shaped to Lead

Rick Warren popularized the SHAPE profile which assesses five ministerial capabilities: Spiritual Gifts, Heart, Abilities, Personality, and Experience.[122] Though many other variations are now available, each personal dimension relates to leadership and equipping.

- o **Spiritual Gifts**
  - As a spiritual organization, the church functions best as members exercise their spiritual gifts within the body (1 Cor. 12). In my estimation, a person with virtually any spiritual gift can attain a certain level of leadership. However, maximum effectiveness largely results from spiritual giftedness complemented with other ministry competencies. Leaders should be familiar with their own gifts as well as those with whom they serve and lead.

- o **Heart**
  - What motivates you to serve and sacrifice? All of us have interests, hobbies or passions that stimulate us to study more, think longer, plan ahead or even change our lifestyles. We have concerns that keep us up at night, and burdens that we carry. We hurt with those who hurt, laugh with those who laugh and run with those who run. Whatever captures our attention then stirs our hearts; these passions are at the heart of our leadership quest. (Psalm 37:4)

- o **Abilities**
  - Many of us have natural abilities such as music, athletics, languages, math or interpersonal skills to be used for God's purposes. Equippers must maximize natural abilities to lead well, honor God, and expand His Kingdom. Through education or training, we can enhance our abilities, strengthen our weakness, and develop new skills.

o **Personality**

- Each of us has a distinct personality. According to Ted Engstrom, "personality is …what sparks the vision and enthusiasm and fuses diversity into unity."[123] We must know ourselves and our people to effectively equip.

  What personality type are you? A bold risk taker, a loyal follower, a gregarious connector, or a conscientious worker? If you understand and embrace your unique personality, you will be able to lead better with a greater awareness of yourself and others. Alone we are incomplete. We need each other, and God designed it so.

o **Experiences**

- Experiences within the context of our family of origin, religious upbringing, romantic relationships, social groups and educational opportunities determine our worldview, our biases, and our values.

Perhaps the most understated element of the SHAPE profile is experience, which is mutable but impactful. Experiences that shaped my ministry skills fit into the following three categories:

Divine Encounters/ Supernatural Moments

God placed influential people in my life who changed me forever: providential appointments scheduled in the heart of God to benefit me and those I served. Movements of the Spirit in corporate worship, an individual spiritual awakening, or serendipitous manifestation can impact us significantly. Whether a salvation experience, a call to ministry or just a spiritual renewal, the sense of the divine is inescapable and transformational. See 2 Corinthians 3:17-18.

Deliberate Decisions

The toughest or most significant life decisions are forced upon us during seasons of transition. A cascade of decisions overwhelms us as we progress through adulthood, attending college, selecting a major, making academic goals, pursuing jobs or a career, finding a marriage partner, starting a family, buying or selling a home, or planning for retirement. The decisions we make influence our present and determine our options and opportunities in the future.

Debilitating Circumstances

No one is immune from tragedy. Decades of pastoral experience in the church cement that reality. The sudden death of a parent, spouse, or family member; the birth of a special needs child; an onset of Alzheimer's; a disabling accident; physical or sexual abuse; and catastrophic house fires, floods or hurricanes are just a few examples. Debilitating circumstances come when they are least expected and the effects may last a lifetime. No one is immune and no one is ever fully prepared. They reshape us as we respond to them.

## ESSENTIAL COMPETENCIES

The effective leader must have an abundance of ministerial competencies. Though there are too many to elaborate upon here, I believe there are four that are essential for the leaders of today and tomorrow.

*Interpersonal Relationship Skills*

Many staff members have lost their position or influence due to weak interpersonal relationship skills. Ministry leaders must be attentive to the people we serve and with whom we serve. Treating others with respect and honor is pivotal to success in ministry. Biblical admonitions to love, esteem, comfort, encourage, and exhort apply to all members of the body of Christ. If we desire our churches to exhibit these fine qualities, we must model them. How can you gauge your own interpersonal skills acumen? First, conduct a personal inventory.[124] Second, look closely at those you lead. Over time, organizations assume the character and qualities of the leader. Developing healthy personal relationships can be an acquired skill and is critical to lead and disciple others.

*Communication Skills*

Have you ever heard or listened to a person who had spectacular ideas but lacked public speaking skills? Perhaps you struggled through a truth-filled manuscript because of poor grammar or distracting writing style? Good communication skills can elevate people, advance ideas, and inspire obedience to Christ. On the other hand, poor communication stifles hearers and repels readers. Jesus was an outstanding communicator. He related to his audience through stories and object lessons. His message was received by the people because it was personal, authentic and authoritative from the overflow of his life and heart. Effective leaders must continually sharpen speaking and writing skills.

*Conflict Management (Resolution) Skills*

Conflict is inevitable. Even happily married couples disagree at times. For some, it is an art form. Unfortunately, the church has long been an environment for squabbles, fights, and divisions. I wish it were not so. The source of conflict is usually deeper than the superficial symptoms present. Leaders must learn to discern the true motives of men, hidden agendas and silent hurts. Congregations riddled with conflict ruin their witness, discourage followers, and diminish their capacity to fulfill the Great Commission in their communities.

Unity is a paramount value for followers of Jesus. In his final prayer in John 17, Jesus prayed specifically for unity among those who would follow. Paul exhorted churches to preserve unity and the bond of peace. Jesus also said our love for one another would distinguish us as believers. How can we love one another and be embroiled in conflict? Equippers must become first-class peacemakers.

*Strategic Thinking Skills*

I am surprised regularly to learn how few leaders are able to strategically plan and execute. Too many leaders are unable to assess their current situation, identify and articulate God-honoring goals, and plan steps for accomplishing those goals.

Strategic thinking can be learned and practiced. If you naturally think this way, the church needs you. If not, take on some small goals, map out plans, enlist people to help, and accomplish tasks. Skills we learn in small venues we can be applied to larger ones.

## CONCLUSION

From my perspective, all ministers are called to disciple and lead so that they influence others to fulfill the Great Commission. We must prepare to hand off the burden of responsibility, the power of authority and the mantle of leadership to the next generation. We must let love lead the way, which is easier when undergirded by a sound biblical and philosophical foundation.

1. Are you committed to the mission personally and organizationally? What actions would enable you to focus more intentionally on the Great Commission?

2. Remember the circumstances when you felt called into ministry. How does that call motivate and sustain you in the

face of difficulty? How has your ministry changed during your service?

3. Have you pursued a Christ like character and attitude? How are you reinforcing Christian character in your church or ministry? Identify one or two areas which you need to exercise caution.

4. Of the four listed ministry competencies, which are your strongest? How have they influenced the priorities in your ministry? Assess your weakest competency. How can you strengthen or compensate for it?

"Work out your own salvation with fear and trembling. For it is God who is working in you both to will and to work according to his good purpose." – Phillipians 2:12b-13 (CSB)

Consider yourself a disciple leader. In other words, you are a follower, adherent, and learner of Jesus. And you are a person of influence with responsibility to lead. You are a disciple leader. The aim of this book is to help you learn, grow and apply the principles. It begins with learning and valuing basic discipleship principles in your personal and church life. Take the orthodoxy of this book and make it orthopraxy. This means you take the biblical and foundational truths that guide our beliefs and convictions on discipleship and implement them into your personal and church life. This should be the practice of your life.

Since you have read through the first eight chapters, you have learned about Spiritual Formation, Cultural Context, Evangelism, Mentoring, Small groups, Serving, Preaching, and integrating Discipleship and Ministry Leadership. These chapters were written with a design in mind. The topic of the chapters represent elements, platforms or approaches for discipleship. Since we all learn, consider the human growth process, beginning with God's creative design for all people to be formed spiritually. Then you progress through the impact of the learning environment, the teacher, the learner, and the curriculum. This process starts individually and advances to a church discipleship strategy to equip believers. It begins with you as a Ministry Leader.

"The ball is in your court." Those are familiar words that describe the personal challenge to take the truths that are evident, the things that you have learned and put them into practice. I've heard those words from coaches, parents, and friends. For the context of discipleship, those words symbolize God's expectations for us. And the good news for us is that God is with us in full partnership to fulfill this challenge given in Matthew 28: 20. Hopefully after reading part one of this book, the challenge to take personal responsibility for making disciples is now highly valued in your heart and mind. Consider this question. Can you begin to organize your personal life around the discipleship of others? Now, can you begin to strategize how to take the personal discipling mandate and create a corporate church strategy? Suggestions on a variety of approaches are found in part two of this book.

As you begin part two of this book, you will find that the chapters are organized around specific church ministries, based on age and gender. The church is multigenerational and representative of all peoples. Due to developmental concerns, there are methods that are more appropriate for preschoolers, children, youth, college-aged, and seniors. There are also more effective discipling methods for men and women due to God's creative design. Leading these church ministries necessitates leadership. In these chapters you find specific and practical suggestions for churches of any size. Now be a disciple leader.

## CHAPTER 9

# MINISTRY LEADERSHIP WITH CHILDREN

## Faye Scott

*"According to God's grace that was given to me, I have laid a foundation as a skilled master builder; and another builds on it. But each one should is to be careful how he builds on it." -1 Corinthians 3:10*

God calls children's ministry leaders to lay down a strong spiritual foundation upon which children can build a solid faith. The foundation of a building is a critical component of the structure. The foundation ensures that the weight of the building is spread evenly over the ground and underneath so that it will not shift or crack under pressure.[125] A building without a strong foundation will eventually collapse.

A couple of years ago, the empty lot next to my home was purchased. Shortly thereafter, I was getting ready for work when I heard a commotion outside. I live on a relatively quiet street so this amount of disruption was quite unusual. Looking out the door, I saw a large crane, a large truck loaded with long, round wooden poles (pilings), other commercial building equipment, and several crewmembers. Minutes later, the foreman of the construction company knocked on my door to advise me that they were about to begin the foundation work by driving those long, wooden pilings deep into the ground. He assured me that they would monitor the seismic activity as the driving progressed.

As I left home for work later that morning, I made the obligatory New Orleans U-turn on my street and caught a glimpse of the pile driver supporting a long wooden pile ready to strike the first blow. I stopped to take a picture of the scene, not knowing how it would be used for ministry, but knowing in my heart that it would be. Now, two years later, I am using it in this book and chapter as an analogy for laying a spiritual foundation.

To begin, the word *foundation* should be defined. Webster defined the word *foundation* as "the underlying base or support; especially the whole masonry substructure of a building; a body or ground upon which something is built up or overlaid."[126] The purpose of a foundation is to secure a building in place and to transfer building loads into the ground.

Before construction can begin, the soil must be analyzed for load bearing capacity. If the soil and groundwork is not stable or thick enough to support heavy loads, a deep foundation is required. Driving vertical structures several feet below the ground's surface provides a stable surface upon which the building can safely be built. The depth of the foundation is determined by how far down the stable soil is beneath the surface.[127]

In 2005, my entire New Orleans neighborhood was approximately six to eight feet under water in the aftermath of Hurricane Katrina. Some structures were destroyed while others remained structurally sound. What determined which buildings stood and which ones washed away? Those homes with a solid foundation were able to better withstand the force of the rushing waters that poured into the city of New Orleans.

Because of frequent hurricanes, homes built in New Orleans now must be able to withstand 130 mph winds. Homes in this area are tied to the ground by attaching structural supports to wooden piles driven many feet into the ground. The structural floor foundation is then attached directly to the piles. This type of foundation is called a pile foundation and is the most common in southern or coastal areas like Louisiana where high water, silt, and loose clay ground content is often found.[128] *The Constructor* outlines the purpose and importance of the foundation,

> "A building will always move when it is built. It can sink, rise, slide or combine these motions. The foundation ties the different parts of the building together so that it does not sink unevenly and crack. Foundations also anchor the building to prevent its moving sideways when, for example, it is built on sloping ground."[129]

Perhaps you are wondering how pile driving in south Louisiana relates to children's ministry. Allow me to explain. Several years ago, I attended a conference in which the leader referenced 1 Corinthians 3:10. As she read the verse aloud, I visualized what our children's ministry should look like! How could it be that I had never *heard* that verse before? A meeting with our Children's Committee a few days later provided support to implement this verse through both the organizational and physical structure of our children's ministry. The basis for the children's ministry at my church is now built around 1 Corinthians 3:10.

God calls children's ministry leaders to skillfully and carefully construct a solid spiritual foundation upon which children can build their lives so that their faith is not shaken when the storms of life arise. The remainder of this chapter is built around 1 Corinthians 3:10. As you read, consider the children's ministry in your own church. How is the ministry providing an immovable spiritual foundation for those involved?

## GOD'S GRACE

My personal call to ministry reminds me of Exodus 4:10-12, CSB when God called Moses to be His spokesperson to the nation of Israel. Moses did not surrender easily, and he argued, "Please, Lord, I have never been eloquent—either in the past or recently or since you have been speaking to your servant—because my mouth and my tongue are sluggish." The Lord said to him, "Who placed a mouth on humans? Who makes a person mute or deaf, seeing or blind? Is it not I, the Lord? "Now go! I will help you speak and I will teach you what to say."

The Lord used this passage to confirm my calling into ministry years ago. I voiced the same arguments to God that Moses did. I did not grow up in the church and felt completely inadequate to answer God's call. The truth is that no one, by his or her own ability, is worthy to teach spiritual truths to children, but God, in His infinite grace, calls us to be His representatives.

## LAYING THE FOUNDATION

Jesus told a parable of the wise and foolish builders in Matthew 7:24-27. One man built his house on sand and another built his house on solid rock. When the wind and rising waters came, the house built upon the sand "fell with a great crash." Jesus said of the house built upon the rock, "The rain came down, the streams rose, and the winds blew and beat against that house, yet it did not fall, because it had its foundation on the rock."[130] Note two things in this passage: (1) The foundation of the house was determined *before* the house was built, and (2) the type of foundation played a critical role regarding the survival of the house. Jesus makes it clear that a house without a strong foundation will not last. The strongest home is the one that is built upon the solid foundation of Jesus Christ.

I have spent some time defining the purpose of a physical foundation and reviewing the methods used to construct such an immovable base, but what does a spiritual foundation actually look like? Characteristics of such a foundation could include the following elements:

1.  The foundation is carefully planned and well implemented.

2.  Knowledge and understanding of scripture are accomplished through the use of age-appropriate teaching principles.

3. Individual needs of students are considered.

4. Students are taught sound biblical doctrine. In addition, because students understand *why* they believe the doctrines of their faith, they are able to withstand an assault upon their own spiritual beliefs.

5. Students possess a clear understanding of the doctrine of salvation and are confident of their own salvation.

6. Students are able to articulate spiritual beliefs in their own words and make a correct application of these beliefs.

7. Programming is strategically and purposefully selected.

8. Leaders and parents work together to meet the spiritual needs of children.

## THE EXPERT BUILDER

We learned earlier that contractors do not haphazardly decide on the type of pilings used in a project. The soil is analyzed beforehand, the depth of the bedrock is determined in advance to determine the depth of the pilings, and the seismic activity is monitored throughout the entire process. No part of the plan is left to chance; rather a detailed, organized plan is implemented. Children's ministers should follow this example, know the spiritual needs of those they shepherd, and know what is important for children to learn and believe. Steve Adams wrote,

> "The ultimate destination of children's ministry is to lead children toward spiritual health. No leader should leave up to chance the spiritual formation and health of the kids in the ministry. We have been given a responsibility and opportunity to influence

the spiritual health of children at a time in their life when they are more teachable and pliable than at any other point in their life. This should not be a random approach, but rather an intentional process that guides our children along the spiritual journey as God prepares them to fulfill their individual and unique destiny, and they reach their full potential as disciples of Christ."[131]

Therefore, an organized approach to accomplish these goals and to continuously monitor the implementation of the process is vital.

No one can know the storms of life a child will encounter in his lifetime. Will he or she experience the death of a loved one or perhaps the divorce of his or her parents? Will he or she experience betrayal from someone they trusted or rejection by someone they respect? Will he or she be bullied? Each of these storms is significant and, without a strong spiritual foundation, can cause the significant damage, if not the total destruction, of a child's trust in the Lord.

As mentioned, the type of pile used in foundation work depends upon the type of soil and the design of the building. More than one type of pile can be used in the same project. Therefore, it can be deduced that there is more than one way to lay a strong spiritual foundation in the life of a child. One form of discipleship may be effective for one child but may not significantly impact the life of another child. The needs of each particular church must be analyzed before the work begins.

Paul wrote in 1 Corinthians 3:10 that we should become expert builders. Your congregation trusts you to know about children and their spiritual needs. They entrust their most prized possession to your care on a regular basis, believing that you are equipped to lead. Parents will come to you seeking advice on parenting, relationships, and spiritual matters, and your leaders will want someone trained to lead them. Simply having a heart for children is not enough. James wrote, "Not many should become teachers, my brothers, because you know that we will receive a stricter judgment." (James 3:1, CSB) James explained that those who teach will be held to a higher standard. We should not take lightly the responsibility of leading in children's ministry. Become an expert builder. Reflect upon the following guidelines and include others in the discussion:

- Determine in which areas you are considered to be an expert builder. Ask yourself why you consider yourself to be an expert builder in that area.

- Determine which areas of leadership might need improvement. Figure out those areas, and then develop a strategy to acquire the necessary skills.

- What training should you receive? Training can be achieved by attending conferences on the local, regional or national level. Online training is readily available and is often free. Podcasts are another excellent source of training. Check with denominational leaders for training opportunities.

- What books or ministry support should you read? Access relevant information through children's ministry books, websites, magazines, and other publications.

- What formal education are you pursuing? Professional vocational education is available through seminary classes in the traditional setting and other venues, such as hybrid and online classes. Many students serve as lay leaders or in bi-vocational or part-time positions. Serving in the local church provides the opportunity to immediately implement what you are learning.

- How are you equipping other leaders to become expert builders? Laying a foundation also means allowing others to be engaged in the building process. One person can build a house, but the process is very slow and the outcome may be less desirable. Learn how to delegate responsibility to others.

- How are leaders trained and supported? Provide regular, in-house training and support for leaders. Provide opportunities for outside training as well. Network with other leaders in the area to provide training.

- What tools are provided for your leaders? Provide resources for leaders to teach effectively. Budget and utilize resources wisely.

## SOMEONE ELSE IS BUILDING ON THE FOUNDATION

Jana Magruder referenced the partnership between the church and families in her book, *Kids Ministry That Nourishes: Three Essentials of a Healthy Kids Ministry*. She wrote that "As we seek to partner with parents and caregivers to truly disciple a child's heart, it's important that both families and churches understand that, ultimately, our God is in control. He calls our children to Himself in His own time. We can teach them the gospel and, more importantly, display the gospel to them, but cannot transform their hearts on our own."[132] Just as a solid foundation is not achieved through the use of one solitary piling, the construction of a solid spiritual foundation requires a team of people working together.

Regarding the house that was built next to mine, the owner told me that he designed the home so that it could withstand hurricane forces. The three-story home is set on a four-foot deep concrete slab that is anchored to the pilings driven into the ground. The successful construction of this foundation required more than one piling. Those who invest in the life of a child – Bible study leaders, mentors, parents, chaperones – all play an important role in laying a deep spiritual foundation for the life of a child.

Each foundation is unique in that its own particular design is dependent upon the blueprint of the structure that will be built upon it. Likewise, each child is unique and has a different set of needs. The spiritual foundation for one child may not be adequate for another child. Analyze the needs of those in your ministry and equip others to meet those needs.

Several crews were utilized through the various stages of the foundation construction of my neighbor's home. The construction work was not rushed, and sometimes there would be no activity for days. The construction foreman told me that they were allowing the foundation to "set" before additional stress was added to it. They wanted to be confident that the foundation was strong enough to support the edifice for which it was designed.

A strong foundation is laid so that a solid structure can be built on top of it. The construction of any structure does not stop with the foundation. Similarly, children do not remain children forever. In the early stages of faith development, teaching should focus on concepts that can easily be understood by literal-minded children, such as the Bible, God, Jesus, the church, and family. Lifeway's Levels of Biblical Learning shows the progression of a child's ability to understand spiritual truths at each stage of development. [133] These progressions of faith development enable children to have a clearer understanding of Jesus and God for salvation.

Each stage of life should be able to rest upon the foundation laid in the early years of a child's foundational faith development. Each stage may provide the child with a deeper understanding of spiritual truth, but the fundamental doctrines of his or her faith should not change with each stage of life.

## BE CAREFUL HOW YOU BUILD

Jesus gave stern warnings in Matthew 18:6 (CSB) to those who would lead a child astray. He stated, "But whoever causes one of these little ones who believe in me to fall away—it would be better for him if a heavy millstone were hung around his neck and he were drowned in the depths of the sea." Two years ago, the youth minister in our church was convicted of inappropriate conduct with one of the girls in our youth group. His crime shook our congregation to the core. Young people, parents, and staff were all devastated. This terrible betrayal of trust could have destroyed the faith of our young people. Parents could have pulled their children from the church. Instead, we witnessed our church family come together and support one another. Make no mistake, however, these were dark and difficult days. The church body had received a strong spiritual blow, and, although the attack did cause some large cracks which required repair, the "structure" did not collapse. The foundation of the body of Christ had not shifted and the church as a whole remained intact. In Genesis 50:20, Joseph said to his brothers, "You intended to harm me, but God used it for good to accomplish what is now being done, the saving of many lives." The only good that came of this tragedy is that our church implemented and faithfully adheres to strict policies concerning volunteers and employees working with minors. Background checks were routinely run on volunteers prior to this incident, but this travesty catapulted the church to a new level of security regarding the care and instruction of minors. What one person intended for bad, God used for good.

Erik Erikson's Psychosocial Stages of Development identifies a series of eight stages of development by which individuals must navigate successfully in order to achieve healthy emotional development. In Stage One, *Trust vs. Mistrust,* the infant develops a sense of trust with interactions that provide reliability, care, and affection or, conversely, a sense of mistrust when these needs are not met. As the crisis of *Trust vs. Mistrust* must be successfully resolved before a person can move to the next stage of development, this stage is crucial in the ongoing healthy psychosocial development of individuals.[134]

When children participate in activities associated with the church, they should be able to trust that care has been given to screen those individuals who are working with them. Parents should feel confident entrusting their children to our care and our teaching, having confidence that they will be well cared for physically, emotionally and spiritually. Once mistrust is born, spiritual leaders may never have the opportunity to build a spiritual foundation as any teaching received from that source cannot be trusted. Meeting the physical and emotional needs of a child is the first layer of the foundation and allows others to build upon that foundation of trust.

Jesus warned His disciples in Matthew 19:14 (CSB) to "Leave the children alone, and don't try to keep them from coming to me …" Since those who lead children are held to a high level of accountability, great care should be taken in leading children. The warning is clear: Be careful how you build. Be careful to whom you entrust the care and teaching of children. Some practical steps to ensure children are safe might include:

1. Screen volunteers carefully. Run initial background checks on volunteers and employees and repeat this process every two to three years. Implement application and reference checks into the recruiting process. Provide job descriptions. Create, provide and implement policies for those working with minors. Search online for forms that other churches utilize.

2. Implement appropriate teacher/student ratios. Children should never be left alone with one adult. Cancel an event if adequate supervision is not possible.

3. Provide sexual abuse awareness training. Some insurance companies provide free access to this training on their website. Check with denomination leaders for available training.

4. Create an emergency operations plan for incidents such as bad weather, active shooter, fire or another emergency. Familiarize leaders and parents with the policies. Practice the plan.

5. Don't rush. Involve new volunteers slowly. Test them with a small responsibility before placing them in a role that carries significant influence. Are they faithful to carry out their responsibilities? How do others respond to their leadership? Do they have a teachable spirit? Do they hold themselves accountable to others?

6. Test doctrine. Application forms provide the opportunity to discuss the leader's salvation testimony and doctrinal beliefs.

## THE SHEPHERD

My personal philosophy of ministry is based upon Psalm 78:72 (CSB), "He (David) shepherded them with a pure heart and guided them with his skillful hands." Notice that David *shepherded* with "integrity of heart". A few months ago, I was in India on a mission trip when I spotted a large number of sheep being led by a single shepherd along a busy highway. The sheep did not stray from the shepherd, because they trusted him to keep them safe. The shepherd, likewise, knew that he could trust his sheep to follow him. Clearly, this was not the first time he had led his flock. The shepherd had built a foundation of trust with his sheep before he led them onto this busy highway! The first layer of the foundation, which is trust, begins when we build relationships with and understand the flock entrusted to our care.

As mentioned, David had "integrity of heart". The Pulpit Commentary says that David "performed his task of governing Israel faithfully." He sincerely sought to do the right thing for his people. He avoided ungodly counsel and strived to avoid anything that went against God's principles. He was a man of integrity, though he was by no means perfect. A minister must be a person of integrity. He must hold himself accountable to others. His primary concern should be to build up the Master's kingdom, not his own.

The text goes on to say that David led with "skillful hands". Barnes says David "was not only an upright and faithful king but also a 'skillful' or prudent one. He built up his kingdom into an empire without suffering any serious disasters."[135] David did not lead his people haphazardly. He used his resources wisely and sought godly counsel. He administered the government with integrity and uprightness. He was skilled and equipped to carry out his calling.[136] We would do well to follow David's example to shepherd with integrity and skill.

# CONCLUSION

When Erik Erikson died, he was in the last state of his Psychosocial Development Theory, which is Stage 8: *Integrity vs. Despair.* In this stage, senior adults age sixty-five and older reflect back on the accomplishments of life either with a sense of closure and satisfaction or with a sense of despair over what was not accomplished. In 1997, Erikson's widow, Joan Erikson, added an additional stage, *Gerotranscendence.* She proposed that in this final stage senior adults age sixty-five and older begin to look forward rather than backward and experience a decrease in fears about life and death.

Erikson's first and last stages of the Psychosocial Development Theory represent the "bookends" of life. One can conclude that the only way a person can successfully resolve the last stage of development is by building a firm spiritual foundation. When an individual enters this last stage of development, it is too late to build a solid foundation. That foundation must already be in existence. May we, as children's ministry leaders, do all that we can to ensure that those entrusted to our care have a firm spiritual foundation upon which they can successfully navigate the storms of life. Reflect upon the following questions:

- Describe the spiritual foundation you are striving to implement for children, leaders, and parents.
- How would you describe your goal to a new leader in your ministry or to a family visiting your church?
- What steps are you utilizing to achieve that goal?
- How does your programming enhance spiritual growth? What method of evaluation is used to determine that there is growth?
- Could your church survive a sexual abuse incident? What are you doing to ensure that it could? Or better yet, that it never has to survive something as horrific as this crime?
- What precautions do you have in place to ensure that children are safe in your ministry?

## CHAPTER 10

# MINISTRY LEADERSHIP WITH STUDENTS

## Jonathan Denton

"We get at most five or six years of ministering to our students. Let's leverage those years with the goal of our students leaving our ministries ready to make disciples in college, in their future families, and in their grandchildren." Jonathan Denton

Every Christmas break, we take our high school seniors and college students on a college ski trip. I learned to ski when I was a teenager and college student, and I love teaching others to ski. Skiing provides opportunities to cheer when students conquer a slope and to laugh uncontrollably when they wipe out. Some of my best memories have been watching students who think they are Bode Miller resemble Frosty the Snowman by the time they reach the bottom of the hill!

Skiing offers something unique that that very few other trips offer and that is the chance to teach students to a new skill that can only be taught by someone who is a more advanced skier than they are. In almost every other sport and activity, the students look more like the experts than the adults. We had the brilliant idea once to have the adult workers play flag football against the winning student team of our flag football tournament. On the first play, three adults were injured, one having a pulled groin, one with a sprained ankle, and one with a torn calf muscle. Yet, on the ski slopes, the students are looking for someone to help them to get down the slope without dying. While it might be fun to watch, a responsible leader cannot just give a student who has never seen snow a set of skis and say "I'll see you at the bottom!" I often wonder if this is exactly what the discipleship of students has become in the church. A student who accepts Christ is then put in a small group and expected to be ready to go on an international mission trip at the next opportunity. It is no wonder why so many youths crash on the difficult slope of adolescence.

After a few ski trips, we learned that the best way to help a student to safely ski difficult slopes was to pair them with individuals who would lead them on this journey. The first step was to have students take a group ski lesson from a professional skier on the slopes. Then, more experienced skiers would spend the first afternoon and next day skiing with the beginners, teaching them what they had learned. Usually, by the third day, everyone was skiing down the difficult slopes that had looked so daunting that first time down the mountain.

I wonder what it would look like if we created a culture of discipleship in our student ministries. What if we had a team of adults who would help a student down the slope of adolescence, teaching the student what they learned and the skills to help them do it themselves? What if students departed our ministries and began to make disciples in their ministries, in their families, and throughout the world? How do we create a ministry like that?

## A CULTURE OF DISCIPLESHIP

When driving up to a ski slope, it becomes quite evident that you are in a different culture, especially if you have just left the Deep South. Everyone is dressed in warm clothes and Northface jackets. On the slopes, the language and accents are also different. People use terms such as front side, goofy, grab, and other skiing terms. The workers are laid back and the town moves at a slower pace. Snow is valuable and has a huge economic impact. All of these things make up the culture of that area.

Now, picture yourself walking into your student ministry. We walk into our ministry spaces so often that we forget what it might look like to others when they walk into our space. A good practice to do periodically is to walk into your space when visitors arrive and look around the area as a visitor would. What culture do you experience when you enter? What do people look like, what do they talk about, and what things are valued?

Many different cultures exist today in our student ministries. Some ministries are built around an entertainment culture. In a this type of culture, everything revolves around the experience that the students have in a ministry. The lights are set to the mood of the service, the drums are loud, and the leaders are dressed in flannel and skinny jeans. Some ministries are built around the family as a whole. Families are championed and do everything together. Some ministries are built around philosophy and theology. These students are great at Bible knowledge and defending their faith. Other ministries are missional, and students are motivated to change their society.

All of these ministries offer great opportunities to lead students to Christ and grow them in their faith. No matter what ministry model you choose and regardless of your mission statement, what does your discipleship culture look like? The answer to that question extends beyond ministry models and mission statements. The culture of discipleship that you establish is vital because it develops the path that will help students to grow from unbelievers to believers on a mission. It develops the path that your students will follow from junior high to the day they leave your ministry and walk onto their college campuses or their first places of work. The discipleship culture of your ministry also influences the words that are used on campus, the feel of the environment, and the attitudes and actions of your volunteer workers.

What then does a discipleship culture look like in student ministry? Psalm 78 gives a great picture of this culture. The psalmist stated in verse 4 (CSB), "We will not hide them from their children, but will tell a future generation the praiseworthy acts of the Lord, his might, and the wondrous works he has performed." First, we must create a place in which the next generation hears about the glory of God, comes to know Him, and learns about His character and work.

Second, the psalmist continued in verses 5 and 6 (CSB), "He established a testimony in Jacob and set up a law in Israel, which he commanded our fathers to teach to their children so that a future generation—children yet to be born—might know." By creating a discipleship culture, we must think through the story and commands of God that we want students to hear. We can use a curriculum so that students will leave our ministries understanding the whole story of Scripture and where they fit into that story. We train adults, both parents and youth workers, to know their testimonies and to be able to share with the students. Kristi, our pastor's wife and one of our discipleship leaders, taught us that, "vulnerability leads to vulnerability." As we share our story of the gospel at work in our lives, students begin to open up about their stories and their need of the gospel.

Finally, we must create a culture of not just student disciples, but also student disciple-makers. The psalmist stated that the goal was not for spiritual transformation in our children, but in the generation that the disciples of our children will disciple. The psalmist's goal was to impact three generations of disciples. While impossible to evaluate, one of our major goals in student ministry is to lay the groundwork of discipleship three generations later. We get at most five or six years of ministering to our students. We must leverage those years with the goal that our students leave our ministries ready to make disciples in college, in their future families, and in their grandchildren. One person who discipled me, Dr. Allen Jackson, once told me, "Discipleship is not complete until the disciple becomes the disciple-maker"[137]

## THE YOUTH WORKER AS DISCIPLEMAKER

Before describing the practices of disciple-making with students, it is wise to stop and examine youth workers themselves as disciple-makers.

Youth ministry has had too many failure stories of its leaders. I believe there are several factors that lead to this. One reason may be that when a person wants to serve, an easy place to put them is on the youth team. The thought is that youth are more independent than children and need less guidance, and it gives the youth worker a chance to try ministry without messing up the adults. While youth ministry does give people a great opportunity to learn ministry, the fault comes when the youth leader or volunteer is not spiritually mature enough to handle the task of discipling students.

A wise saying regarding discipleship is that "you can't lead someone to a place you have not been yourself." Student ministry leaders must place a great emphasis on the character of their youth workers. In his study of adolescents, Chap Clark found that "By the time children, even the successful ones, reach high school and middle adolescence, they are aware of the fact that for most of their lives they have been pushed, prodded, and molded to become a person whose value rests in his or her ability to serve someone else's agenda."[138] As disciplers of students, we do not want to add another adult into the life of a student that only has an agenda. Instead, we want leaders with high character to dive into their world and meet students where they are, hear their stories and hurts and lead them into a deeper walk with God that places them on a mission back into their world.

In a recent study done by the Fuller Youth Institute of churches with healthy student ministries, the number one discovery about leaders was not that they were cool, wore skinny jeans, and had great beards, but that they were "warm". The researchers stated, "Warmth often lives much deeper than your programs and structures – It's the lifeblood coursing through the veins of your church body…As it turns out, *warm* is the new *cool*."[139] When choosing leaders to disciple students, one must look for leaders who genuinely love God and love students. Sometimes they are flashy, but often they are simple, ordinary adults that have been transformed uniquely by the gospel. They need to be someone who lives out their faith in a genuine way and disciples students, not because it adds to their service resume, but because they genuinely want to see students grow in their relationship with God.

## PREPARING THE PATH

When I plan to visit a new place, the first thing I do is grab a map. My wife is constantly embarrassed by my looking at maps. She prefers to just punch it into her phone and let her phone tell her all the directions. I must first look at a map so that I can get the overall picture of where everything is. Even if I put the address into my phone, I still zoom out so that I can see all the turns. When you look at the whole map, you can see the start and finish, and then determine the different turns that need to happen.

Looking at the whole map also helps you to avoid dangers. In skiing, the trail map is very important because it shows the difficulty of the slopes. My wife gets really upset with me if I take her down a slope that is too difficult for her. In order to keep our marriage peaceful, I will memorize the map and take a trail map with me on the slopes so that every turn we make is on the correct slope.

Before discussing the specifics of discipling an individual student, it would be wise for us to think about the overall map of discipleship. The overall picture helps us to plan for discipleship to occur and to minimize potential problems. While we love to talk about "organic" and "life-on-life" discipleship, this only occurs when we have a plan in place. Three things are important to consider as we look at the overall picture of discipleship.

First, we must consider the age-graded path that our students will take in our ministry. Instead of waiting until the first Sunday of each semester to determine what we will teach, it is wise to map out a three- to six-year teaching plan that will cover the whole Bible. We want each student to leave our ministries with a solid understanding of Scripture.

Second, we must develop programming elements to fulfill our mission statements. Each element should be different than the other elements. If not, then students will simply choose one programming element. You may reach 90 kids total, but only 40 students show up at any given time. Each element should also be one aspect of your mission statement so that you can track their growth as they move through your programming.[140] For example, the mission statement at my previous church was "Bring them In, Build them Up, and Send them Out." In order to fulfill the mission statement, I designed our midweek service to primarily be a "bring" service. At this service, students would regularly hear the gospel and we would design most of what we did to connect with the students. We then designed our Sunday mornings to be a "build" program element. We would use this service to get students into the Word of God and teach them skills to study the Bible for themselves. Our final programming elements were our "send" elements. We used the student choir and discipleship groups to train students in worship and prepare them to live missionally, both in their individual daily lives and throughout the country and world.

Third, make certain that you have a plan in place for the days following a student's salvation experience. We realized that we celebrated a student's salvation, but then saw many who fell away after a few months or years because our discipleship was designed for advanced growth, not new growth. Luckily, we have seen a recent growth of resources for first time believers. Find a resource or design one yourself, and make these available for students when they accept Christ. When I met with a student for baptism, I gave them the new believer resource and then either I or a leader close to them would meet weekly with the student for four weeks to review the study from the previous week and answer any questions they might have about their new walk with Christ.

## DISCIPLING INDIVIDUAL STUDENTS

After creating an overall map for discipleship, we must then leverage opportunities to disciple individual students in their walks with God. The beginning chapters of this book have great information on the specifics of discipleship. A few things that I want to highlight in the area of discipling students is the importance and power of intentional discipleship groups, small and gender-specific groups, a designed plan of study, and a designed endpoint.

First, it is important to provide opportunities for intentional discipleship groups. If we do not create space for discipleship, it rarely happens. We decided to use Sunday nights as our discipleship time and created groups for 6-8 weeks that centered on a discipleship topic. These short-term groups allowed students to begin to test-drive discipleship. For those that we identified as Faithful, Attentive, and Teachable (FAT, a term I learned in college from Campus Crusade for Christ)[141], an adult would reach out to these students and ask them if they would be interested in meeting weekly for a year or two. Many times, these groups would meet before or after school. Your process might look different, but are you creating space for discipleship to happen? Often, this means cutting a program or an event so that time and space are created for discipleship.

Second, the discipleship of students happens best when the groups are small and gender-specific. We limited our groups to three to five students. If it is less than three, the group will be too small if one person misses. The group tends to never gain consistency to meet because the meeting keeps getting canceled every time one student misses (and they will because they are teenagers). If the group has more than 5, then not everyone gets to talk and you miss a big component of discipleship: transparency.

Gender-specific groups are also important because of transparency and openness. Teenagers, as well as adults, are less transparent when the opposite gender is in the same room. The two genders also have different issues that need to be addressed in discipleship. Regarding gender, we also found that a group of three to five is important for openness as a teenage guy typically does not open up in front of a big group of guys. A small group is helpful for a teenage girl because as she hears other girls being transparent, she will typically become transparent as well. Sometimes, she will be more transparent in a group than she will be one-on-one with an adult because of her longing for community (and also because meeting one-on-one with an adult can feel awkward).[142]

One of the great things about the renewed emphasis on discipleship is that more and more resources are becoming available every day. Almost every major youth curriculum company has a discipleship curriculum now. By looking at the scope and sequence, you should be able to find a curriculum that matches your aim in discipleship. The curriculum we chose had an emphasis on missional living each week, which is what we hoped our discipleship groups would be. Also, make certain that the curriculum places a great emphasis on getting students into the Bible for themselves through spiritual disciplines. While there are a wide variety of topics that can be covered, one of the best gifts we can give to students is to help them understand the authority of Scripture and its application in their daily lives.

Finally, having a designed endpoint for discipleship groups is important. In student ministry, we often think of this as graduation. For some groups, that might be a perfect end. But for many, two to three years in length is a good general rule. After two or three years, the discipler tends to lose focus and energy, the curriculum plan tends to finish, and the disciples are often ready to be trained to lead others. Another strength to limiting the groups to two-three years is that students are exposed to more adults during their time in student ministry. Research shows that the more significant adults a student has in their life, the stronger their faith tends to be. Richard Ross states, "Students who have heart connections with at least five significant, spiritually alive adults have the best opportunity to develop a sustainable, alive faith embracing the supremacy of Christ."[143] Finally, a predetermined end date helps groups to end strong by giving them a goal and not just fade off like so many tend to do.

## SOME WISE ADVICE FROM DISCIPLE-MAKERS

I want to end this chapter by sharing some quotes from several youth leaders who have done a great job discipling our students. I hope you enjoy these great words of wisdom:

- Be available. Students benefit from multiple godly adults in their lives.

- Be consistent. Meet with them regularly and live a life that matches what you say.

- Be prepared. Students can spot a fake and unprepared person a mile away.

- Having a group of students from different grades was really effective because you consistently have growth because as one student graduates, a new student comes in

- Model the importance of Scripture memory

- Fellowship as a group once a month at least

- At each meeting, share a struggle and a victory and help them devise a plan to help overcome their struggle

- Make sure to have time for prayer each week

- Study the Bible together teach them to rely on His truth, not just books

- Listen to a podcast or song at the beginning or end of time together

- Send them a scripture and thought for the day

- Do life with them and go to their functions

- Find a way to spend one on one time with each individual student at least once a quarter

- When discipling another person, always make sure that your own walk with the Lord is pure. Even the parts that people can't see.

- If you are being discipled, first choose to humble yourself. I think the main thing that keeps people's hearts closed to other's constructive criticism or discipling is pride.

- The actions of our lives as followers of Christ are COMPELLED by the love of Christ. Everything we do, everything we say, is driven by the person and story of Jesus Christ.

- Never underestimate the community cultivated by FOOD and SPORTS when discipling and interacting with youth.

- Youth (youth and people in general) want to know and be known. Be INTENTIONAL in seeking to know the person with whom you are in discipleship.

- Don't do all the work for them. Let them take some ownership.

- Lastly, time. Whatever we spend most of our time on, is probably what we care about most. This can go both ways. Whether you're being disciple or disciplining another, be proactive by setting aside time for that on a weekly basis.

## CHAPTER 11

# MINISTRY LEADERSHIP WITH EMERGING ADULTS

## David Odom

You are all a lost generation.

> – Gertrude Stein in *The Sun Also Rises*
> by Ernest Hemingway

We used to play pretend, give each other different names
We would build a rocket ship and then we'd fly it far away
Used to dream of outer space but now they're
laughing at our face
Saying, "Wake up, you need to make money"
Wish we could turn back time, to the good old days
When our momma sang us to sleep but now we're
stressed out

> – Twenty One Pilots, *Stressed Out*

Brad and Veronica are getting married. Their two friends Gerome and Tasha are excited to attend the wedding. The four met in college and stayed close over the years. As the four friends turn 23 this year, the approaching wedding of Brad and Veronica places a spotlight on the stark differences between them.

Brad started dating Veronica sophomore year and they have been together for five years. Brad is still in school working on his MBA and Veronica is an elementary school teacher. Their friends see the pair as the perfect couple and affectionately refer to them as "Braronica."

Gerome and Brad are best friends. They have a lot in common, such as their love for basketball and playing video games. However, they have significant differences as well. Gerome dropped out of college after sophomore year. He says he just doesn't know what he wants to do with his life. When Brad and Veronica moved in together, Gerome moved back into his parent's house. After having four jobs in the last three years, he is currently unemployed.

Tasha and Veronica were roommates freshman year. Tasha briefly dated a guy in college and got pregnant. She has a four-year-old son, Micah. As a single mom, she relies heavily on her parents to help care for Micah while she works as a nurse technician. Even though she is employed, Tasha is considering her parents offer to move back home to share expenses. She is cautiously optimistic about the future, but she is tired of feeling "in-between" adolescence and adulthood.

Tasha is the only one of the four friends who is a Christian. She stopped attending church after high school. However, her son now attends preschool at her old church, and this prompted her to return to her faith. She now attends a women's Bible study on Tuesday nights.

Brad, Veronica, Gerome, and Tasha represent a sampling of young adults in our world today. Young adults today either are single, married, divorced, employed, unemployed, have kids, have no kids, live independently, or live at home. This chapter will help leaders develop a vision and strategy for ministering to emerging young adults by identifying key indicators of spiritual maturity as well as suggesting four areas of ministry focus: relationships, community, mentoring and teaching. However, let us first look at young adult development.

## YOUNG ADULT DEVELOPMENT

A discussion of young adult development begins with defining what it means to be a young adult. It may seem obvious to most, but from a discipleship and ministry perspective, it may not be so clear. For example, does adulthood begin at age 18 or 21? Should college students be included in youth or adult ministries? Do we include singles in our adult ministries or assume everyone is married or will be married? What about young adults who do not feel comfortable in a college Sunday School class because they have dropped out of school? The journey from the teenage years toward full adulthood is often a time of confusion, anxiety, and frustration. Many young adults feel disoriented, hurt, and damaged.[144] Leaving home, getting married, and becoming financially independent are among some of the milestones linked to traditional adulthood. However, increasing numbers of young adults postpone achievement of these markers. How leaders choose to define and organize ministries to young adults, has a far-reaching impact.

Developmentally, young adults acquire thinking and social skills that set them apart from children and adolescents. Cognitively, young adults have developed higher reasoning and critical thinking skills.[145] From a psychosocial perspective, some young adults may still struggle with the adolescent stage Erikson describes as a search for personal identity. According to Erikson, the goal of young adulthood is establishing relational intimacy.[146]

The definition of adulthood from an educational perspective is persons "whose age, social roles, or self-perception, define them as adults."[147] Margaret Lawson believes that individuals reach adulthood when they become "personally accountable for themselves and accept adult responsibilities."[148] The challenge is whether or not some young adults identify with such definitions.

Another way to define adulthood is through a series of markers. Traditional markers of adulthood include accepting responsibility for oneself, making independent decisions, and becoming financially independent.[149] However, there is growing evidence to suggest that these traditional markers no longer apply to many of today's young adults – that in fact, they are *not* fully adult at all.

## EMERGING ADULTHOOD

Developmental psychologist Jeffery Jensen Arnett identifies people between the ages of 18 to 25 as new classification he calls *Emerging Adulthood.*[150] According to Arnett, emerging adults feel they are experiencing an in-between period of life. They have left their teenage years, but they have not become adults. It is the first time in history that people in their younger twenties are not considered adults.[151]

Arnett's research suggests several reasons for the development of emerging adulthood. Among them are shifting moral beliefs and the invention of the birth control pill that fueled the sexual revolution of the 1960s.[152] Young people in their late teens and early twenties were encouraged to engage in sexual activity outside of marriage free from public guilt or shame.[153] Today over two-thirds of American young adults cohabit before marriage.[154]Other sociocultural changes contributing to emerging adulthood include a dramatic growth in higher education, delaying of marriage, and a willingness of parents to extend financial support through the twenties.[155]

Prolonged financial support by parents can lead some to have a skewed view of the value of work. For instance, some emerging adults may feel entitled to only work in jobs that are meaningful and rewarding. However, if they lack skills and formal training, emerging adults may only find low-paying hourly jobs that are not personally fulfilling. Also, young adults can view a job as a temporary "gig" rather than a career path. As a result, young adults on average change positions seven times between the ages of 20 and 29.[156]

Another defining characteristic of emerging adulthood is the lack of adult experiences which starts in high school. Tim Elmore has found that teenagers spend most of their time with peers (about 60 hours a week) and only about 16 hours with adults.[157] Richard Ross reflects on these stats by observing that for most of human history, the opposite was true. "Through the centuries, children 4 and older spend most of their time performing chores. They learned to do adult-like tasks by working side-by-side adults."[158] The result was that by the time teenagers became adults, they had been relating to and observing adults for most of their lives. However, this is rarely the experience of today's young adults.

One way to understand the differences between today's emerging adults and previous generations is to compare two versions of the popular board game *Life*.[159] The game developed by Milton Bradley in the 1960's is quite different from the current version.

Table 5: The game of LIFE then and now.

| Then | Now |
|------|-----|
| Linear game board from young adulthood to retirement | Four loops to choose from: Earn It! Learn It! Live It! Love It! |
| Nine career and salary cards | Twenty-seven career cards and seven promotion cards |
| Paper Money | Visa card |

The original version of *Life* forced players to choose one of two paths to adulthood: college or work. The linear nature of the game required players to progress through school or work, marriage, childbirth, home ownership, and retirement.

The modern version of the game replaces the linear nature of the game with interconnected loops that players enter and re-enter throughout gameplay. Also, there are more career opportunities from which to choose. These differences demonstrate how the journey from adolescence to adulthood has changed over the years. The remainder of this chapter will use the terms young adult and emerging adult interchangeably to refer to the same age group.

## GENERATION Z

Complicating a review of the developmental aspects of emerging young adulthood is the fact that a new generation of students is entering this age group. Over the last decade, discussions of young adults have centered on Millennials. However, Generation Z (born 1996-2010) is following on the heels of Millennials, and they will soon make up the majority of emerging young adults. The oldest of this new cohort is entering their twenties.

Research on this new generation has centered primarily on market and educational research. Here are a few of the findings: [160]

- Daily interact with 3 to 5 screens (compared to 1-2 for Millennials)
- Highly entrepreneurial (72% want to start a business)
- Lower attention span (8 seconds—down from 12 seconds in 2000)
- Communicate with images (photos, emojis, gifs, etc.)
- Concerned for the planet
- Want to create media, not just view it

Gen Z students also have a fear of missing out (FOMO). They are relational and collaborative and desire participatory learning experiences. Today's emerging young adults also differ significantly in spiritual belief.

## FAITH DEVELOPMENT

Forty-one percent of young adults attend weekly religious service.[161] However, only 8% would name a clergy has a role model. Emerging adults have a pluralistic ideology and superficial theology.[162] Christian Smith, the lead researcher for the National Study of Youth and Religion, discovered that the spiritual beliefs of most teenagers and young adults do not match traditional Christian faith. Smith describes their belief as Moral Therapeutic Deism.[163] The core tenets of this belief system are:

- a God exists who created and orders the world and watches over human life on earth
- God wants people to be good, nice, and fair to each other, as taught in the Bible and by most world religions
- the central goal in life is to be happy and to feel good about oneself
- God does not need to be particularly involved in one's life except when God is needed to resolve a problem
- good people go to heaven when they die

These statements express the dominant religious worldview held by most emerging adults. Ross explains that as a result most people ages 18 to 25:

- are not prepared to walk in faith all their lives
- do not live in intimate relationship with Christ
- do not value the glory of God above all things
- do not embrace a love relationship with the local church
- are not committed to completing the Great Commission—locally and globally
- do not stand ready to live—or die if so called—to see Christ's kingdom come on earth[164]

The faith of emerging young adults is weak and anemic. Kinnaman asserts that "the next generation is caught between two possible destinies—one moored by the power and depth of the Jesus-centered gospel and one anchored to a cheap, Americanized version of the historic faith that will snap at the slightest puff of wind."[165]

This weakening of faith typically begins in high school. Although teenagers today are among the most religiously active, by the time they reach age twenty, they are the least religiously active.[166] Emerging adults who drop-out of church fall into three categories:[167]

- Nomads who walked away from church but still consider themselves Christian.

- Prodigals who lose their faith and label themselves as "no longer Christian."
- Exiles who are invested in their Christian faith but feel stuck between culture and church.

Emerging young adults are the least represented group when it comes to church bible study. [168] They increasingly feel alienated from the church. As a result, as many as 60% stray from their faith in the college years. [169] What is fueling emerging adult alienation from the Church? David Setran and Chris Kiesling demonstrate that both emerging adults and the church share the blame.

Table 6: What is fueling emerging adult alienation from the Church.

| Emerging Adult Factors[170] | Church Factors |
|---|---|
| 1. Life Disruptions<br>   – Moving<br>   – Separating from Family<br>   – New Relationships<br><br>2. Delayed Marriage & Parenting<br><br>3. Educational & Work Demands<br><br>4. Do not Need Church<br>   – Outgrown it<br>   – Download it | 1. Church is Overprotected and Sheltered<br>2. Church is Shallow<br>3. Church is Anti-Science<br>4. Church is Repressive and Maintains Outdated Sexual Standards<br>5. Church is Exclusive & Spurns Non-Believers |

Even if today's young adults do not drop out of the church, they are more likely to have developed an immature faith. Tom Bergler calls this immature faith the *juvenilization* of American Christianity. He defines it as "the process by which the religious beliefs, practices, and developmental characteristics of adolescents become accepted as appropriate for Christians of all ages."[171]

Is there hope? How can we help emerging adults develop maturing faith? The answer lies in a commitment from church leaders to disciple emerging adults.

## DISCIPLESHIP

Church leaders often assume that young adults can grow spiritually on their own. They need leaders who will intentionally engage them to prevent dropout and help emerging adults grow toward spiritual maturity. [172] Kinnaman rightly asserts that the dropout problem is a disciple-making problem.[173] A strategic plan for the discipleship of emerging adults is needed.

As with any ministry, leaders should begin with the end in mind. What is the goal of discipleship? What are the characteristics of a spiritually maturing young adult? The apostle Paul talked about the goal of discipleship in his letter to the Ephesians.

> Until we all reach unity in the faith and in the knowledge of God's Son, growing into maturity with a stature measured by Christ's fullness. Then we will no longer be little children, tossed by the waves and blown around by every wind of teaching, by the human cunning with cleverness in the techniques of deceit. But speaking the truth in love, let us grow in every way into him who is the head—Christ. From him the whole body, fitted and knit together by every supporting ligament, promotes the growth of the body for building up itself in love by the proper working of each individual part. (Ephesians 4:13-16, CSB)

Paul explains the process of spiritual growth in developmental terms. He describes it as the natural progression from infancy to adulthood. According to Paul, maturing faith is strong enough to withstand "every wind of teaching" and "evil scheming." He also describes a person with maturing faith as one who understands his or her place in the body of Christ. To develop maturing faith in emerging young adults, leaders should focus on four growth areas in the church: developing relationships, building community, establishing disciples, and producing disciple-makers.

## DEVELOP RELATIONSHIPS

Rather than implementing a program, a leader's priority should be on building godly relationships with young adults.[174] Jesus focused on relationships. The call to "follow me" in Matthew 4:19 was a relational invitation. Jesus invited his disciples into a relationship with him. True discipleship can only take place in the context of relationships. Leaders must intentionally invest in relationships with emerging young adults. God-centered relationships produce faithful and mature disciples.[175]

To build relationships, church leaders should initiate interaction with emerging adults. Fellowship time in both formal and informal settings is needed. Formal settings include church Bible studies and other ministry-related gatherings. Informal settings include lunch meetings, gatherings after work or school, and at sporting events. In the context of these relationships, young adults develop a sense of community.

## BUILD COMMUNITY

A community of believers is essential for spiritual growth. Leaders must help emerging adults see the value of being part of a community of believers in a local church. The following are three reasons to develop community.

First, community is biblical. Christ died for the church (Eph. 5:25). The writer of Hebrews teaches that believers are to make community a priority by not neglecting to meet together (Hebrews 10:25). Christians develop community as they pray for and support one another (Acts 2:42-47, Gal. 6:2). Serving together is another biblical component of community. Believers serve God using their gifts in the church (Romans 12:4-5).

Second, community is vital to spiritual growth. Emerging adults need godly fellowship and accountability for faith to mature. The church community creates a sense of family.[176] This spiritual family provides security, stability, and accountability.[177] They experience transformation in social settings.[178] Emerging adults learn as they pray with other believers, read scripture aloud, take notes, sing together, share feelings, hurts, and doubts.

Finally, community promotes a sense of belonging. Community is the context for intentionally communicating values, commitments, and lifestyles.[179] Leaders can promote community discipleship through small groups, activities, and service projects. Ultimately it is not the theological conversion that leads to regular church attendance but rather relationships and community.[180] The goal of community building is to establish disciples and lead them to become disciple-makers.

## ESTABLISH DISCIPLES

Leaders establish disciples by leading emerging adults into a saving relationship with Jesus Christ and giving them the spiritual food necessary for growth. In the church, this is expressed through evangelism and Bible study. Young adults need regular engagement in both areas to spiritually mature. They are cyclical – evangelism leading to Bible study and Bible study infoming evangelism.

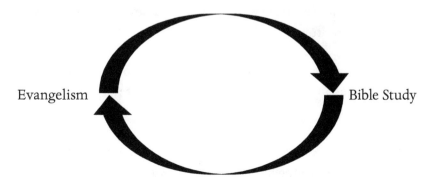

Evangelism     Bible Study

The first element is evangelism. Church leaders must develop a strategy for clearly presenting the gospel to emerging adults. What are the steps to becoming a Christian? What scripture passages describe sin and Christ atonement? Memorizing these elements allows leaders to be ready to share with emerging adults at moments notice.

In addition to key verses describing how to become a Christian, leaders should also prepare for questions and doubts. Apologetics is a term used to describe a defense of the faith. Leaders should become familiar with apologetic responses to questions such as: How do we know the Bible is true? Is Jesus the only way to a right relationship with God? Why is baptism important?

A reasonable response to these other questions will help leaders to witness to emerging adults, but a personal relationship of mutual trust is the key. That is why building relationships and community are vital. Many of today's emerging adults want a sense of belonging before they believe. Relationships provide a safe environment for questions and doubts related to salvation.

The second element to establishing disciples is Bible study. Biblical illiteracy is a growing problem among emerging adults.[181] Research shows that they also lack a deep understanding of their faith.[182] Studying the Bible helps young adults learn about God and leads to spiritual wisdom.[183] It also helps emerging adults realize their identity in Christ and understand their purpose. Leaders should remember these five characteristics of effective Bible study with emerging adults:

1. Start with the basics – Where did the bible come from? What is the difference between the old and new testaments? When was it written?

2. Study systematically – Choose a book-by-book/verse-by-verse approach or a topical study that moves through the Bible by subject

3. Go deep – Study theology and don't be afraid ask hard questions that allow young adults to wrestle with ideas.[184]

4. Make it visual – Emerging adults respond to images and graphics that depict spiritual concepts[185]

5. Be personal – Curriculum is important, tools do not make disciples. God uses His people to make disciples. [186]

Discipleship should lead to transformation. One method for helping emerging adults experience transformation is called *narrative discipleship*. Nathan Byrd describes narrative discipleship as a process to assist emerging adults to "identify themes in their journey of faith in order to establish a foundation for transformative learning to occur."[187] It helps them connect the dots. The basic process involves directing young adults to write down their testimony or faith journey. This testimony is their narrative of faith. Then young adults are encouraged to share moments of their faith experiences in a group setting. The process of telling their stories provides a context for emerging adults to reflect on faith. [188] As their faith develops, young adults need to be encouraged to become disciple-makers.

## PRODUCE DISCIPLE-MAKERS

Effective churches produce disciple-makers. It is not enough to merely focus on discipling emerging adults; leaders must focus on disciples who produce disciple-makers. Producing disciple-makers happens through evangelistic training and the godly example of a mentor.

Lead young adults to share their faith with others as a natural result of their discipleship. Teach the same steps to become a Christian that leaders learn. Train emerging adults to share their own story of how they became a Christian. Challenge them to engage in gospel conversations their peers. Demonstrate how to make disciples in the context of relationships.

The unique relationship between mentor and mentee provides a strong basis for discipleship and disciple-making. Learning from the example of others is a model used throughout scripture – older believers mentoring younger believers.

- Mentors lead by example – they model Godly behavior and biblical morality.[189]
- Mentors reveal God's work in the lives of mentees[190]
- Mentors work life-on-life because, in the end, spiritual growth is "hand-crafted," not mass-produced.[191]
- Mentors provide an opportunity for accountability.[192]

Leaders must intentionally match emerging adults with a mentor. Emerging young adults are often isolated from adults.[193] As a result, it limits the kind of advice or counsel they receive.[194] They often do not have relationships with older and wiser believers.[195] Leaders must recruit disciple-makers who demonstrate faithfulness, reliability, and dependability.[196]

## CONCLUSION

Brad and Veronica's wedding provided Tasha an opportunity to talk about her faith with her friends. Her discipleship training helped Tasha articulate her beliefs and answer some of their questions about Christianity. She encouraged the bride and groom to attend a Bible study at her church for young married couples. Tasha also encouraged Jerome to start meeting weekly with a ministry leader at her church. Jerome is not yet a believer, but he is increasingly open to faith.

As leaders develop relationships, build community, establish disciples, and produce disciple-makers, emerging adults will grow and be built up in love (Ephesians 4:16). These growth areas will help them develop a maturing faith. Prayer, preparation, and implementation of these elements can lead to effective ministry leadership with emerging young adults.

**Questions for Personal Reflection**

What is your plan for building relationships with young adults?

In what ways are you providing opportunities for emerging adults to learn together in community?

What is your discipleship strategy for teaching and training emerging adults?

Who is mentoring young adults in your church? Who could be?

## CHAPTER 12

# MINISTRY LEADERSHIP WITH ADULTS

### Bert Ross

Developing adult leaders is a lot like planting a vegetable garden. When you plant a garden, you have the end results in mind, which are usually fresh home-grown vegetables. My favorite vegetable was tomatoes. I love tomato sandwiches with mayonnaise and my wife makes the best homemade spaghetti sauce. I could easily go to the grocery store and buy them, but there is a profound sense of joy and fulfillment when I go through the process of growing my own tomatoes. The benefit of working outside as a form of mental health is also an added bonus to gardening. Healthy ministries and organizations are led by leaders who understand the difference between interacting with those you lead and engaging with those you lead.

Harvesting the fruit of a garden is not accomplished overnight. It is a year-long process of creating the right circumstances or culture for a healthy harvest. To grow a successful vegetable garden, one must be willing to engage with the process. We had to work with our hands tilling the soil, moving rocks, watering when needed, applying fertilizer, getting dirty, and being willing to sweat. A successful garden requires three aspects from the gardener: the heart-willing to work in the heat, hoeing the garden, and pulling weeds; the mind- understanding how plants grow, when to water, when the fruit is ready to pick, and how to preserve and freeze the vegetable or fruit to enjoy later, time and patience because it is a process. I learned to grow vegetables from my grandfather and my father-in law and others who grew vegetable gardens.

It took years for me to learn all they knew and a willingness to be engaged in the learning process. I had to commit to be with them in the fields where the process of growing vegetables took place. When you buy vegetables from a grocery store, you only interact with someone else's process and are never aware of the process it takes to get the vegetables into the grocery store. Most ministries and churches approve of the development of adult leaders in the same manner. They want to interact with someone else's process and challenging work when it comes to developing adult leaders. They are looking for an effortless process that can be accomplished in a few meetings or hours and are not willing to be disciplined in the work of equipping ministry leaders.

## CORE VALUE OF LEADERSHIP DEVELOPMENT

The lack of leadership development and empowerment of adults in the church is a growing issue. One of the most difficult challenges for ministries and nonprofit organizations, today is attracting, keeping, and developing talented emerging leaders. Churches need to view adult leadership development as a core value of the culture and focus of the ministry. The complexities and challenges of ministry today demands innovative ways of thinking and leading. The question is how to develop these innovative approaches to leadership. More than ever before, ministry leaders are required to be active and skilled disciples. Churches and ministries must intentionally give time and finances to achieve this goal. Leadership development is a process, not just a onetime training event. It allows the emerging leader to apply what he has learned in order to develop his skills. Sadly, few ministries do this and for most ministries, it is a declared value, not a real value, and they cannot produce visible results. Empowering volunteers and future leaders provides them with opportunities to make their own decisions regarding their ministry tasks and daily impact as a leader. Typically, the activities most correlated with high engagement and empowerments are not always the tasks that receive the most attention by church leadership in the daily ministry of the church. The focus must be on developing the abilities and skills of potential leaders as they seek to mature as a disciple and achieve the goals of the church. Churches are looking for a leader with the skill set, character, and capacity to fit the right ministry role as perfectly as possible.

## BEGIN WITH THE END IN MIND

In the development of the twelve disciples, Jesus began with the end in mind. When Jesus began to call leaders for the future, He called ordinary men with a clear and compelling purpose to become fishers of men. In Matthew 4:18-22 (CSB) "As he was walking along the Sea of Galilee, he saw two brothers, Simon (who is called Peter), and his brother Andrew. They were casting a net into the sea—for they were fishermen. "Follow me," he told them, "and I will make you fish for people." Immediately they left their nets and followed him".[197] The disciples did not know what being "fishers of men" meant or what process and journey fulfilling the call of Jesus would entail. Developing adult leaders is a spiritual journey. Churches need to develop a strong level of spiritual discernment and accountability as well as to ask God for guidance when seeking new leaders.

## FOUR PERSONAL FOUNDATIONAL PRINCIPLES OF LEADERSHIP DEVELOPMENT

To increase leadership empowerment and development, the leaders of a church must create a culture of leadership development, built on the following four relational and personal foundations:

**Foundation 1: *Authenticity*.** Adults must be authentic and committed to developing a deep intimate relationship with Jesus Christ. Spiritual maturity must be the core reality in a leader's personal life, not a weekly performance of activity or businesses.

**Foundation 2: *Caring*.** Churches must demonstrate genuine care for potential leaders, regardless of their level of leadership. This allows the church to see a person, and not just a body to fill a position.

**Foundation 3: *Trust*.** The church must demonstrate absolute integrity, truthfulness, openness, and trust. Only after a deep level of trust is developed can leadership development take place. People will not be interdependent with others that they do not trust. Trust is built when leaders make deposits of integrity and trust into their people, being consistent to their word.

**Foundation 4: *Transparency*.** For leaders to equip people, those who serve under their leadership must see God working in the life of the leader. A much needed culture change in ministry is for leaders to develop transparency as a character trait. Disclosing information about the inner workings of a ministry and entrepreneurial leadership can create new opportunities for the ministry and can develop future leaders.

## WHAT'S FIRST?

If a church is not promoting volunteer leader empowerment, it will take more effort for volunteers to respond to any leadership. The leadership of pastors and ministry staff is linked to volunteer empowerment and development. When a volunteer leader understands his or her ministry role, the better he or she will be able to contribute to the overall wellbeing of the ministry. The leadership of the church is obliged to create a culture which promotes volunteer and leader empowerment. Several questions that leaders must ask as they develop a culture of leadership development are as follows:

- What does the church/ministry culture and experience need to look like, sound like, and feel like?
- How does the position/ministry contribute or fit with the total ministry purpose as a whole?
- What do they want their people to think, feel, and do differently?
- What is the vision of the church/ministry?

## NEW MINDSET

To change the future of leadership development in churches and ministry, leaders must create a mindset that leads to a desire to learn. Churches must create a culture that encourages leaders to embrace challenges and see them as an opportunity to grow. Timely and honest feedback will facilitate learning and improvment. Churches with a true growth culture cultivate a safe place for people to take risks, make mistakes, and learn.

Increasing employee and volunteer empowerment and development correlates directly to a positive impact on key ministry metrics. Volunteer and employee development and empowerment ultimately runs from the top of the leader board down to all leaders. Leaders must model those outcomes and behaviors desired in future leaders. Before any future leader is ever approached for development or ministry involvement, those currently leading must clearly communicate the purpose of the ministry.

## IS MANAGING PROGRAMS ENOUGH TO DEVELOP LEADERS

For churches to create a culture of leadership development, they must understand the difference between leading and managing.

Part of leading is to motivate volunteers and employees to increase the quality and quantity of ministry. Some positive motivational skills used by leaders are communicating a vision, rewarding and recognizing volunteers, and encouraging and thanking leaders. Negative motivational behaviors displayed by leaders include disciplining, threatening, coercing and controlling. When controlling, a leader typically uses monitoring and evaluating activities to ensure that an organizations' goals are being achieved. Many church leaders are excellent at managing the ministry of the church but never actually lead the ministry of the church. In most churches and ministries, leaders focus on managing ministry meetings, such as Sunday school, children's events, worship services, committees, calendar events, budgets, processes, procedures, and paperwork. Leadership, however, focuses on inspiring, leading, and motivating people. Leaders who are developing a culture of empowering people throughout their organizations provide a way to meet core organizational objectives.

Some mistakes that adult ministry leaders often make include failing to lead, not setting clear goals with volunteers, not developing employees and leaders which leads to confusion about priorities, and forgetting what it is like to be a volunteer. An increase in leader and employee development requires an increase in the amount of time spent giving and receiving information. It also requires improving communication within the ministry. Leadership development and empowerment is time-consuming, but can help reduce organizational conflicts.

There are four organizational principles for leadership development which are as follows:

- Shared purpose and values: There must be an alignment between the values, purposes and goals of the emerging leader and the organization. The foundation of developing new leadership is the promotion of consistent vision, mission, and a set of values to the members. The vision and purpose must be so compelling that they want to encourage teamwork and commitment.[198]

- Creative mental development and motivation: The organization must encourage their leaders to be innovative and creative. They encourage innovative ideas from their followers and never criticize them publicly for their mistakes. The leaders focus on the *what* in problems and not on who is at fault. Churches and ministries must be willing to discard any old practice if it is found to be ineffective.

- Intentional influence: The organization must believe that a leader can influence followers only when he practices what he preaches. Leaders act as role models which followers seek to emulate. Such leaders always win the trust and respect of their followers through their action. Leaders typically place their followers' needs above their own, sacrifice their personal gains for them, and demonstrate high standards of ethical conduct. The use of power by such leaders is aimed at influencing others to strive for the common goals of the organization.

- Individualized attention: Leaders act as mentors to their followers and reward them for creativity and innovation. The followers are treated differently according to their talents and knowledge. They are empowered to make decisions and are always provided with the needed support to implement their decisions.

## ONE LEADER AT A TIME

There is no one size fits all leadership development process or program that churches can implement. Leaders are encouraged to use their own skills and abilities, and when ministry volunteers are modeling and living out these values, it becomes a major motivation for others to follow. Good leaders empower their people and their teams by involving them in the overall process of conducting ministry. The development of leaders can occur they are enabled to identify problems, collaborate on solutions, implement their own ideas, and receive credit for their contributions. Leaders must be willing to transfer the decision making of day to day ministry responsibilities to those within the ministry. Effectual leaders identify individual needs and adapt their work to meet those needs.

When working with new employee or volunteers, leaders must understand several key characteristics. First, they are excited, eager, and ready to serve even though they are inexperienced and, in most cases, new to the ministry goals and tasks. They usually do not realize how little they know. Leaders need to be more hands on and concrete with directions, goals, and solutions to the issues they face in leading.

As leaders begin to grow in their knowledge about the ministry, they may find it harder than they expected and may become discouraged and overwhelmed. Leaders must be willing to listen to what is not being said and allow the emerging leader to share their concern. Leaders will need to provide feedback and reassurance on real solutions and allow the emerging leader to be involved with the solution. As emerging leaders gain continued knowledge and confidence, they will begin to demonstrate a greater sense of expertise and confidence but may still need some feedback on ideas and actions plans. [199]

## WHY LEADERSHIP DEVELOPMENT DOES NOT HAPPEN

The empowering of ministry leadership with adults does not take place in the presence of certain leadership styles or in the lack of leadership training. Many times, the leaders unintentionally transfer their influence to others on the team because of their own personal limitations. This may be due to their own inexperience, insecurity, or insufficient training. By maintaining control, the leader inhibits leadership growth and the further equipping of volunteers to accomplish the work of the organization.

Another characteristic of poor leadership occurs when leaders give team members the responsibility of accomplishing a goal without giving him or her the authority to make decisions. In some instances, leaders abdicate their role when they no longer feel accountable for organizational outcomes.

## IT'S FAIRLY SIMPLE

Churches and ministries need to move from a culture of leadership control to one of supporting people to do what they were enlisted into the ministry to do. This change instills an increased sense of accountability in ministry leaders. Creating a leadership development culture requires a new approach to linking ministry success to employee development, empowerment and engagement. Leaders must be willing to be model a culture of coaching. Senior leaders must integrate leadership development within their ministry team areas and reward teams and individuals as they demonstrate new behaviors.

The development of leaders should focus on helping them learn to lead themselves. To ensure self-leadership, the leader must distribute power to others through engagement and delegation, causing them to feel needed and empowered. Leaders must also encourage employees to develop their ideas, gifts, and talents for solving problems and act on their solutions. One of the greatest challenges for ministry leaders is to provide emerging leaders the freedom to realize that what they do matters and that they can make a difference. This allows a worker to own their ministry. Often, the issues of being able to make choices is not due to inadequate leadership but to inconsistent systems and communication. Ministries need to broaden the focus of a ministry position to allow for broader boundaries and agreed upon ministry objectives that can be achieved by the emerging leader. Many ministry roles are vague and poorly developed to help reach ministry goals.

When potential leaders do not have the knowledge, skills, information, or resources to do a ministry effectively, people feel overwhelmed and disabled. Developing the needed skill and motivation is essential for new leaders. When providing training to emerging leaders, the leader is making an investment in that person by offering the knowledge and opportunities for strengthening their skills. If a person has the knowledge and necessary skills for the assigned duties, then the new leaders' confidence increases. Leaders must understand the skill and willingness of the developing person they are mentoring or coaching.

Leaders must also understand that each person matures at a different pace according to their skill level entering the leadership role and their willingness to learn. Each leader learns through individual experiences, the amount of training they have experienced combined with follow up, and the amount of coaching that helps them apply what they have learned. When working with those just beginning a leadership position, the mentor or pastor must be more hands on and instructive. Peer mentoring and coaching is becoming a foundational part of developing leaders. A good coach helps leaders to develop clarity of purpose and focus on action that effects the whole ministry. The value of using a coach is that very few leaders receive honest, open feedback because of the power of their position. The two main coaching methods are diagnosis and development.

The coach uses direct observation, leadership assessments, and personality assessments to diagnose the strengths of the leader, and then helps the ministry leader implement a development plan to measure improvement. Many future leaders are willing to serve in the church and other ministries, and it is therefore essential to provide unlimited information to the new leader. Mentors and those working with new leaders must allow them to be in the center of solving critical problems and contributing to key goals. When new leaders fail or struggle, they face a lack of self-confidence and feelings of helplessness, powerlessness, and crippling self-doubt. The essential elements demonstrated by a mentor for developing a new leader's confidence and competence include openness, concern for their growth, and the ability to trust One of the struggles facing many involved in equipping leaders in the church is accountability. Fostering accountability is essential to developing new leaders. The goal is to get ministry volunteers/leaders to work collaboratively and to trust that others will do their part. It is in peoples' nature to want to please others and meet the expectations of their peers. "Leaders know that part of their job is to set up conditions that enable each and every team member to feel a sense of ownership for the whole job."[200]

When maturing leaders are motivated and empowered, then the entire ministry including ministers, volunteers, and those the church is desiring to reach, will benefit from it. There can be notable improvements in ministry success, time, costs, morale, and efficiency. There may also be a reduction in turnover and absenteeism. A lack of empowerment can result in negative consequences for the organization such as the wasting of time, resources, and money.

## WHEN AND WHERE DID THE LEADERSHIP DEVELOPMENT PROBLEM OCCUR?

Discouragement, lack of involvement and the desire to serve can occur at any time and in any organization or ministry. It is usually evident within an organization when a ministry leader attempts to control and reduce the influence and abilities of a volunteer who serves within a ministry. It must be remembered that ministry leaders are not transferring their power; rather they are sharing their power with emerging leaders and volunteers. When trust is built, not only is the leader given shared power, but they are also given the tools and decision-making power necessary to complete the ministry and task.

In order to transition from poor leadership practices to those which empower others, leaders must be willing to ask the question, "How should the culture be changed?" Leaders should be very clear about the benefits for the ministry, the team, and individuals when they accomplish the goal. They must also be clear about the significance and magnitude of the ministry. Good leaders also demonstrate that they care about all the people in the organization and they show respect for their opinions, their thoughts, and their differences.

## CONCLUSION

If a ministry and its adult ministry leaders develop a culture committed to developing leaders, it will change the beliefs and behavior of ministry volunteers in ways that drive the church to accomplish Kingdom results. Empowered and developed leaders take ownership of ministry concerns, team issues, and overall results of the work. Adult ministry leaders who are engaged and empowered work with passion and energy, driving ministry innovation and moving the ministry onward.

## CHAPTER 13

# MINISTRY LEADERSHIP WITH SENIOR ADULTS

## Loretta Rivers

"Even while I am old and gray, God, do not abandon me, while I proclaim your power to another generation, your strength to all who are to come." (Ps. 71:18 CSB)

One of the greatest joys of my life is teaching senior adults in Bible study. I look forward to Saturday afternoons and Sunday mornings. On Saturday afternoons at 4 p.m., I facilitate a homebound Bible study class, and on Sunday mornings, I lead a Bible study class for women aged sixty and above. The homebound class grew out of a need in my Sunday class, as some members had become physically unable to attend and missed the ongoing fellowship of the group. The homebound class takes place via a telephone conference call, and I never hang up the phone on Saturday afternoon without feeling encouraged, motivated, and grateful. The members testify of God's faithfulness through all the circumstances of life. Recently, when studying Psalm 23, Mickey, a ninety-one-year-old member who faced cancer recently, proclaimed, "I have had a lot of valleys in my life, and I know God is with me. You can't trust God and worry at the same time."

The opportunities for ministry leadership with senior adults abound in the 21ˢᵗ century. As of July 1, 2016, the United States population aged sixty-five and above was 49.2 million persons, or 15.2% of the population.[201] By 2050, the number of persons sixty-five and older is expected to reach 83.7 million, or 21% of the U.S. total population.[202] These statistics signify the importance of ministry to senior adults.

Ministry to senior adults aged sixty-five and older is the focus of this chapter. A review of church websites revealed numerous names for this group, including older adults, mature adults, adults 55+, and Boomers, as well as names which seek to defy aging, such as Keenagers, Young at Heart, and Just Older Youth (JOY). This chapter also includes a discussion of the following: the Bible and aging, senior adult ministry leaders, preparation for ministry with senior adults, and suggestions for ministry with senior adults.

## THE BIBLE AND AGING

The Bible contains many truths about aging adults. First, God created all persons in His image (Gen. 1:26). Life is precious and is to be treasured and valued no matter our chronological age, because God created us and knows the beginning and the end of our lives. According to Psalm 139:16 (CSB), "Your eyes saw me when I was formless; all my days were written in your book and planned before a single one of them began."

Second, God has a purpose for Christians throughout their lives. The psalmist wrote that "The righteous thrive like a palm tree and grow like a cedar tree in Lebanon. Planted in the house of the Lord, they thrive in the courts of our God. They will still bear fruit in old age, healthy and green, to declare: 'The Lord is just; he is my rock, and there is no unrighteousness in Him.'" (Ps. 92:12-15 CSB). For example, God gave Sarah and Abraham a son, Isaac, in their old age. God called Moses at age eighty and Aaron at age eighty-three to lead the children of Israel out of Egypt and into the Promised Land. "Joshua was now old, advanced in age, and the Lord said to him, You have become old, advanced in age, but a great deal of the land remains to be possessed."

(Jos. 13:1, CSB). At age eighty-five, Caleb said, "I was 40 years old when Moses the Lord's servant sent me from Kadesh-barnea to scout the land, and I brought back an honest report. . . My strength for battle and for daily tasks is now as it was then. Now give me this hill country the Lord promised me on that day, because you heard then that the Anakim are there, as well as large fortified cities. Perhaps, the Lord will be with me and I will drive them out as the Lord promised" (Jos. 14:7, 11-12, CSB). Abraham, Sarah, Moses, Aaron, Joshua, and Caleb continued to have work to do in service to the Lord despite their chronological ages.

Third, senior adults deserve respect. Leviticus 19:32 (CSB) says, "You are to rise in the presence of the elderly and honor the old. Fear your God; I am the Lord." We should respect senior adults because of their knowledge and life experiences. The Bible also stresses, "wisdom is found with the elderly, and understanding comes with long life" (Job 12:12, CSB).

Fourth, God provides help to older adults. The psalmist declared, "For You are my hope, Lord God, my confidence from my youth. I have leaned on You from birth . . . Don't discard me in my old age. As my strength fails, do not abandon me" (Ps. 71:5-6a, 9, CSB). Isaiah 46:4 (CSB) records God's assurance to His people, "I will be the same until your old age, and I will bear you up when you turn gray. I have made you, and I will carry you; I will bear and save you." As believers, senior adults can always depend upon the promises of God.

Fifth, senior adults have a responsibility to leave a spiritual legacy to future generations who will carry on God's work in the world. The Bible illustrates spiritual heritage in the following examples. In 1 Chronicles 29:28 (CSB), David "died at a good old age, full of days, riches, and honor, and his son Solomon became king in his place." Paul addressed Timothy's spiritual heritage in 2 Timothy 1:4-5 (CSB), "Remembering your tears, I long to see you so that I may be filled with joy. I recall your sincere faith that first lived in your grandmother Lois and in your mother Eunice and now, I am convinced, is in you also." Senior adults who strive to leave a spiritual legacy live with an awareness that someone will continue the work they have done for God.

## SENIOR ADULT MINISTRY LEADERS

A shortage of workers serving the elderly is predicted in many fields, such as social work, nursing, long-term care administration, and physical, occupational, and speech therapy. Significant predictors of working with older adults in a career include coursework related to aging, more frequent quality contact with older adults, lower anxiety about personal aging, and less negative views of older adults.[203] In my own experience as a seminary professor, I have found few students who come to the seminary with a desire to work with older adults. In *A Vision for the Aging Church: Renewing Ministry for and by Seniors*, James M. Houston and Michael Parker stated that they were unable to find any seminary in the United States that comprehensively had reviewed its curricula for aging-related content.[204] Hence, ministerial students most likely lack adequate training to meet the needs of older adults.

Churches fill senior adult ministry leadership positions in a variety of ways. A few churches have a staff person whose responsibilities focus fully on senior adult ministry. Other churches have a staff person assigned senior adult ministry responsibilities along with other duties. Additionally, churches have lay persons that provide leadership to senior adult ministry. Nonetheless, ministers that work with older adults should love older adults, enjoy working with older adults, and value older adults. Ministers should also have a positive attitude, an openness to new ideas, an appreciation for history, and a recognition of what older adults have to offer. In addition, patience, understanding, compassion, and kindness are necessary qualities. Good interpersonal relationship skills, such as listening and problem-solving, are needed as well. Besides developing interpersonal relationship skills, ministers should continue to grow in their knowledge about senior adults. Seminary classes, continuing education opportunities, conferences, and contact with other ministers can provide information, insight, and ideas for ministry.

Ministry leaders should not do ministry alone; they should be continually searching for others to recruit and train for service. Ministers have the responsibility of "equipping the saints for the work of ministry" (Eph. 4:12, CSB). Providing training opportunities, access to resources, and ongoing support are vital to the success of the senior adult ministry. Ministers should also be regularly involved in giving spiritual guidance and ensuring spiritual needs are addressed through the various activities of the senior adult ministry.

Senior adults should also be involved in leadership. Without senior adult involvement, a minister risks planning great programs that will be attended by no one. Senior adults have the ability and experience to provide leadership in ministry. Many churches have a senior adult council, or leadership committee, that meets regularly to plan activities and give guidance to the senior adult ministry.

## PREPARATION FOR MINISTRY WITH SENIOR ADULTS

Ministry leaders should prepare prayerfully for work with senior adults. Seeking God's guidance and direction is necessary in working with older adults. In planning for ministry, the following recommendations may be useful.

Ministers should examine their own views about aging, death, loss, and grief. Is aging viewed as optimistic or pessimistic? A minister's views about aging likely will influence their work with older adults. In addition, ministers need to be comfortable with death, loss, and grief. Working with senior adults will most certainly bring opportunities to minister to those who are dying and to those who are grieving. People may approach ministers with ethical issues about living wills and end-of-life care. In addition to death-related losses, some senior adults experience losses related to declining physical and mental health, relocating to a new living situation, and relinquishing the car keys which signals an end to independent mobility.

In addition to considering their own views about aging, ministers can help to combat ageism, "the stereotyping and generalizing about people on the basis of their ages."[205] Some common misconceptions about older people include they are old and sick, they complain about everything, they are unwilling to change, and they use too many of society's resources. Some people believe that a church is dying if most of its members are over the age of fifty. Senior adult ministers can confront these myths and stereotypes about older adults by providing accurate information and giving examples of older adults who do not fit stereotypical molds.

Following the examination of attitudes and beliefs, ministers may find a ministry inventory helpful in determining who the senior adults in their church and community are and what ministries and services are focused on meeting their needs. A ministry inventory can be tailored to meet the needs of each church and may include a demographic study of the church and community, surveys of church and community members, interviews with leaders who serve older adults in the church and community, and focus groups that consider issues relevant to senior adults. The ministry inventory documents the needs of older adults and identifies resources available to meet those needs. An inventory often provides the names of older adults who need ministry or specific areas, such as nursing homes, assisted living facilities, or retirement communities, where ministry is needed. In addition, completing a ministry inventory helps to strengthen or establish relationships with senior adults and leaders of community agencies and develop a list of referral sources for the church.

Another component of the ministry inventory is an assessment of church facilities to determine if they are aging-friendly. Some questions for this assessment include the following: Are parking spaces close to buildings designated for senior adults; Do buildings have ramps or zero-step entrances; Are location signs easily read; Are restrooms handicap-accessible and close to meeting locations; Do hallways and meeting spaces have ample lighting; Are hearing assistance systems available; Do chairs have armrests that provide support when sitting or standing; and Do floors have non-slip surfaces? The facilities assessment, along with the other parts of the ministry inventory, can be used to help determine priorities for future ministry with older adults and to decide a direction, such as whether building on existing ministries or developing new ministries is the best option.

In addition, spending time with older adults offers valuable insight.

Ministers who invest time in getting to know the older adults to whom they minister are more likely to be accepted and effective as ministry leaders. The optimum way to learn about senior adults is by spending time with each adult. Listening to an individual's story provides a better understanding of that person. When individual time is not possible, ministers can take advantage of group opportunities, such as Bible studies, weekly meetings, and fellowship gatherings, to interact with older adults. Furthermore, a survey of older adults can be useful in gathering a list of needs, interests, and resources.

In planning ministry, ministers must be aware of the great diversity that exists within the older population. A one-size-fits-all approach will be inadequate. Older adults differ according to race, ethnicity, cultural identification, gender, family composition, education, work status, income, social roles, values, and generational cohorts. Other differences include functional ability, personal interests, personality, health status, living arrangements, religious beliefs, and friendship patterns. Purposeful ministers find ways to creatively minister to diverse groups of older adults.

Some ministry leaders find generational differences to be a great challenge. Older adult ministries potentially span three generations. As the Baby Boomers age and lack interest in participating in traditional senior adult ministries, churches are seeking new approaches to reach this generational cohort. Although a thorough examination of generational differences is beyond the scope of this chapter, ministers that recognize the need for a variety of ministries targeted to specific needs of each generation will have greater success in reaching all older adults.[206]

In addition to focusing on different generations, ministry intentionally should involve men and women. Churches may have a tendency to offer programs that appeal more to women. Men often are more difficult to engage than women, but, once engaged, men can be faithful participants. Some possible avenues to involve men include recreational trips, activity-based volunteer opportunities, intellectual studies, and challenging mission projects.

Church leaders should consider the extent to which current ministries adequately meet the needs of all senior adults. Ministers should avoid abrupt changes in existing ministries which can be difficult for older adults. When change is necessary, involving older adults in the decision-making process can facilitate understanding and cooperation. When senior adults know that they are valued and their opinions are respected, they are more likely to be supportive of changes.

## SUGGESTIONS FOR MINISTRY WITH SENIOR ADULTS

Implementation follows careful preparation. The following suggestions for ministry with senior adults are offered for the minister's consideration. Senior adult ministry should focus on meeting the needs of the whole person - spiritual, emotional, physical, and mental. First and foremost, senior adults need a relationship with God. We cannot assume that chronological age or church attendance equals a relationship with God. Ministers should assist older adults in assessing their spiritual conditions. Some senior adults need to accept Christ as personal Lord and Savior and follow Him in believer's baptism. Discipleship is essential following salvation and can often be accomplished through ongoing Bible study groups in the church. Finally, ministers should encourage senior adults to utilize their spiritual gifts in service to the Lord.

An effort should be made to include senior adults in every aspect of the church. Senior adults are a vital part of a church congregation. Senior adults can volunteer, pray, contribute financially, participate, and provide encouragement. Senior adults can serve in leadership positions and on committees and ministry teams. Intentional ministers help ensure that senior adults are aware of, and hopefully involved in, all areas of ministry within the church.

Second, God created human beings with a need for relationships with one another. Senior adults want to feel emotionally connected to others. Recent studies have linked loneliness and social isolation with increased risk for health problems and death.[207] Older adults may experience loneliness and social isolation due to the death of a spouse, moving to a new location, or decline in functional ability. The church has a unique role in addressing the relationship and emotional needs of older adults. Bible fellowship classes, weekly church activities, and service opportunities provide occasions for ongoing social interaction.

Ministers can also promote involvement with older adults through publicizing opportunities for ministry and service. For example, intergenerational connections offer many positive occasions for meaningful relationships in the church. Mentoring and reverse mentoring programs give older and younger generations opportunities to invest in each other. Although intergenerational interactions should not be forced, ministers can create environments for these relationships to develop.

Furthermore, churches can help meet the physical needs of older adults and positively impact their health. More people in the 21st century die from chronic diseases than acute infectious diseases.[208] The rise in deaths due to chronic disease has led to a focus on wellness. Churches can provide exercise programs, health fairs, health education, nutritional classes, support groups related to weight loss and specific diseases, and information and referral services to community resources. In addition, churches can provide healthy lunches and snacks for older adult activities.

Churches can also assist in meeting the mental needs of older adults. Intellectually challenging activities that encourage seniors to build upon existing knowledge can be beneficial. For example, a short course in Biblical archaeology or early church history could renew interest in studying familiar Bible passages. New experiences likewise offer opportunities for enrichment.

Some senior adults face mental health challenges, such as depression, anxiety, and addiction. Ministers should be alert to changes in behavior and attitude that might signal a problem. Familiarity with community mental health resources will enable ministers to assist senior adults in times of crises.

Vulnerable populations of older adults should not be forgotten. Vulnerable populations include institutionalized and homebound elderly, older adults with dementia, never married and widowed men and women who live alone and have no family members, and persons aged eighty-five and above. If people cannot come to the church, the church must go to them. A Bible study for homebound adults is one example of the church reaching out to senior adults who cannot attend. A possible format for a homebound Bible study is five minutes of welcome, introduction, and church news; thirty to thirty-five minutes of Bible study; and five to ten minutes of sharing and prayer time. The recommended group size is ten to twelve members. The group needs a facilitator/teacher. The teacher should enlist group members individually in person, if possible. The teacher should inform prospective participants of the purpose of the group, explain the format of the group time, provide any guidelines for the group, and give instructions for participation in the group. Some adults may need assistance from a family member or friend. Participants only need a phone and a quiet place to participate. The church can mail large print Bible study materials to participants every quarter. Contact is maintained with group members through telephone calls, visits, and cards. In addition, ministers should assist homebound and institutionalized adults to find ways to continue utilizing their spiritual gifts despite physical limitations.

Technology can be useful in ministry with older adults. Live streaming worship services, using teleconferencing for Bible study, and relating through Facebook and other social media help older adults maintain vital connections to the church. Intergenerational ministry opportunities are available when younger members of the church are willing to teach older members how to use technology.

Ongoing contact with senior adults is essential. Ministers can maintain contact through letters, phone calls, text messages, visits, and social media. Scheduling opportunities for regular contact and maintaining a database of interactions with brief notes can aid in the fulfillment of this important task. Furthermore, visits to persons in the hospital and those in crisis situations need to be timely.

Ministers can assist senior adults in facing fears associated with aging. Some fears of older adults include retirement, economic security, purpose and meaning of life, family relationship issues, illness, and death. Reassurance of God's presence and practical support from the church can aid in confronting crisis situations.

Senior adults should be valued and appreciated. Churches should acknowledge the valuable contributions of older adults. Some churches recognize senior adults annually on the first Sunday of May, during Older Americans Month. Giving senior adults the opportunity to share their testimonies or tell about volunteer experiences allows others to learn from their faith journeys and service involvement.

Ministry with senior adults opens the possibility for ministry with several other groups of people, including caregivers, family members, and geriatric professionals. Some senior adults reside temporarily or permanently in institutions, such as hospitals, prisons, mental health facilities, and nursing homes. In each of these institutions, older adults interact with those providing care for them. While ministers can provide spiritual support for caregivers in institutions, perhaps a more valuable service of ministers is encouraging older adults who have the ongoing contact to share their faith. Ministers can provide Bibles and devotional materials that older adults can share with others.

Ministerial contact with family members of older adults and geriatric professionals is also likely as each is concerned with providing care to senior adults. Ministers can support family members and professionals through prayers and visits, as well as sharing of resources.

Ministry with senior adults can be a rewarding and fulfilling experience. The challenge to the church in the words of the psalmist is, "Don't discard me in my old age. As my strength fails, do not abandon me" (Ps. 71:9, CSB).

## Questions for Reflection

1. How do you view your own aging process?

2. What have been the joys and challenges in your experience working with older adults?

3. What recommendations would you make for your church regarding ministry with senior adults?

## CHAPTER 14

# MINISTRY LEADERSHIP WITH MEN

## Scott Sullivan

*The way to change the heart of a community is to change the heart of its men.*

-Dr. Jack Graham

My heart aches for men like Jim. Jim was "saved" at age 13, but, like many teenage boys, he was mischievous. One blistering summer afternoon, Jim was caught stealing a gumball machine from the police station. After a quick phone call from the sergeant, Jim's dad showed up and whipped his rebellious 15-year-old son. The embattled boy was not sure whether his father was spanking him as a lesson or if it was to make his father feel better. Either way, Jim's last words to his dad were, "I hate you!" The next day, Jim's dad, grandfather, and sister were killed in a car wreck.

In college, Jim played football with his best friend, Bo. The last day Jim would ever speak to his friend was on the football field. Jim was supposed to lead with a block to create room for Bo to run. Bo was tackled hard and hit his head on another player's knee just before reaching the ground. Jim ran to his fallen friend only to hear Bo say, "Everything's OK." Two hours later, Bo died.

Everything was not okay for Jim. The losses had left him sad, lonely, and lost. Then he met Linda. He soon married this woman of conviction and beauty. Life seemed great. Jim had the perfect wife, great kids, and an abundance of friends; he was even fishing the B.A.S.S. circuit. But, in December of 1996, Jim was dealt another devastating blow when doctors diagnosed Linda with myelodysplasia, a bone marrow disorder. Six months later, Linda passed away.

Often, the local church does not have a game plan to engage men like Jim. In most churches, a typical men's ministry comprises a half-dozen men who put on a fish fry or big buck contest and then call it a day. Jesus had much more in mind when He called the original disciples to Himself, trained them, and launched them to impact the world for the gospel.

How can the local church mold and mobilize men like Jim with the good news of Jesus Christ? How can the local church provide a ministry to men in such a way that they find what they *need* while they pursue what they *want*? Jesus discipled a small band of men just like Jim to reach the world with the gospel. If the local church fails at anything, it must not be in the discipling of men. Robert Coleman asserts,

> "It all started by Jesus calling a few men to follow Him. His concern was not with programs to reach the multitudes, but with men, who the multitudes would follow. Men would be His method of winning the world." [209]

Many churches are not effectively reaching and discipling men in their community. It is time for church leaders to begin ministering "to" men and stop ministering "at" them. Men like Jim say they are disillusioned with God or see no need for the institutional church. It is futile to try to convince men that going to church on Sunday morning at 9:15 is better than sleeping, fishing, hunting, or golfing. Leaders must focus more of their efforts and time on heart transformation than on behavior modification. Engage men with the gospel of Jesus Christ and the desired behaviors will follow.

Many churches seek to reach men by tracking what men want out of their church experience. There are pointed differences between what men *want* and what men *need*. Men want freedom, but they *need* a purpose. Men want their personal passions stirred, but they *need* peace. Men want the security of retirement, but they *need* the adventure of a daily personal walk with Jesus. Men want to know that they have the ability to succeed at the point in their life when it matters most, but they *need* to find their value in Jesus and learn to live like Christ. The church will never do anything more Christ-like than to engage men in the community and turn them into transformed disciple-makers.

## THE BEST DEFINITION OF DISCIPLE YOU MAY NEVER HAVE HEARD

Every church must lead its men to become transformed disciples of Jesus so that they can then multiply that process among other believers. For that to happen, leaders must identify and promote a biblical definition of disciple. The Greek term for disciple (*mathetes*) generally refers to a "learner" or "student." But the biblical concept of being a disciple of Jesus Christ is much richer than one word. In 2 Timothy 2:1-7, Paul shared three "word pictures" with young Timothy to help him understand that a disciple is a committed, passionate, and faithful follower of Christ. No other place in the Bible does Paul give such rich and clear imagery of what a disciple of Jesus Christ looks like.

First, Paul told young Timothy in verse 3 that a disciple is like a "good soldier." Good soldiers are committed to pleasing their commanding officer. Every soldier comes to a place in his career when he must decide whether to take the easy road or to dig deep and serve out of commitment. Paul wanted Timothy to know that as a man the easy path is rarely the best path. Men in our communities are starved for this type of message with which to connect. Boys in their homes are starved for that type of role model to follow.

Paul then pointed out that a disciple is like an "athlete." Few things are more exciting than watching the passion that is collegiate athletics. Like college athletes, Christians must serve with unmatched passion—like there is no tomorrow. Paul wants Timothy to grasp that there is no greater privilege than to train as a disciple of Jesus and to multiply that experience. Men desperately need to know that they are giving themselves to a task that is God-sized and urgent.

Finally, Paul told young Timothy that a disciple of Jesus Christ is like a farmer. Many in the farming industry understand that the key to successful farming is to faithfully do the work and then trust God for the growth. The benefits of the harvest follow the faithful work of the farmer, but they do not precede it. Paul wanted Timothy to understand that being a disciple of Jesus means faithfully serving and following through on tasks, then trusting God to provide the power to do so. Many men in local churches will serve faithfully and give sacrificially once they hear the gospel and experience heart transformation.

Do not misunderstand Paul's intent. He did not give an exhaustive checklist or a set of rules to follow. Paul did at least two things. First, he challenged the very heart of his disciple. Timothy needed to know that the call of God to walk as a disciple was not easy, but well-worth the effort. That is why Paul began his challenge to Timothy in verse 1 with encouragement: "Be strong in the grace that is in Christ Jesus" (2 Timothy 2:1 CSB).

Paul also wanted Timothy to know that he must shift from being a disciple to becoming a disciple-maker. Four generations of disciples are listed in verse 2: Paul, Timothy, faithful men, and others. The process of being a disciple and living as a disciple-maker never ends this side of eternity. Paul knew that he must replicate the gospel seed Jesus planted in him or the mission would fail to reach its worldwide goal.

The great task of men's ministry leaders is to create a process by which men are trained to become committed, passionate, and faithful followers of Christ. This ongoing disciple-making process must emphasize transformation and multiplication. Life transformation without multiplication brings short-lived success. Replication without life transformation results in the lifeless ministry we see in so many local churches today. What can a church do then to engage men effectively in ministry?

# 4 KEYS TO ENGAGE MEN IN MINISTRY

*Create a Culture of Service*

Men want to know that they are investing in something that really matters. Churches must develop a culture of servant leadership in which men are called to pour their lives into valuable ministry with eternal impact. A leadership culture that points to service before personal gratification must develop organizationally from the top down. The leader of the men's ministry must make a habit of serving others before he can lead his men to do the same. Ultimately, the pastor sets the tone for this type of leadership structure, and the men's ministry leadership team must then model and reproduce the vision.

The men's ministry can do at least four things to create and manage a servant leadership culture that lasts. Leaders must:

- Move men from a mindset of apathy to urgency as they view their ministry field. Leaders can support this by communicating fresh vision early and often to keep purposeful objectives in front of the men.

- Learn to involve as many men as possible, which will broaden the base of the ministry and provide a larger pool for leadership growth.

- Highlight ministry *wins* as they promote a strategic model for men to follow.

- Multiply the leadership impact by establishing new groups for men to connect with and clearly outline how men can connect with these ministry opportunities.

*Create a Pathway to Serve*

Once the pastor and ministry leaders catch the vision of serving others and reaching men, the next step is to create a clear pathway for men to follow in becoming disciple-makers who serve and lead. Patrick Morley wrote that a man wants three things in life: something to give his life to, someone to share it with, and a strategic personal system that helps him to understand why the first two things are important, and so difficult.[210] Too many churches ask men to serve on a team without clarifying what they are being asked to do, what boundaries exist, what goal they are trying to achieve, how much money they have to work with, and to whom they should answer. Vague ministry assignments produce frustration and burnout. Intentional ministry assignments produce measurable results and momentum.

*Centralize Service Opportunities Around the Mission*

Never spend time promoting or conducting ministry projects that provide no eternal value. For example, a men's ministry would be wiser to minister to shut-ins who rarely get cared for rather than spend three months coordinating a fried-fish fellowship for men who in many cases already attend on occasion. A healthy, growing men's ministry will learn to centralize every service opportunity or ministry opportunity around the mission of the church. In other words, be willing to put any function or program on the chopping block if it does not strategically point you toward your mission.

*Celebrate Wins*

Your people will imitate what you celebrate, so celebrate what you want your men to imitate. For example, life transformation is key, so have men share their testimonies. Not only will that produce inspiration, but it will also provide accountability.

Do not be afraid of messy. Sooner or later one of your guys who shared testimony will fail morally. We are not holding individual lives up as models of perfection. We are holding Jesus high as the One who can remedy our imperfections. To see a man come back from failure can prove incredibly beneficial in your men's ministry.

## 5 ESSENTIALS FOR A HEALTHY MEN'S MINISTRY

*Gospel-Centered Ministry*

Men in your community will respond to the gospel of Jesus Christ. Once they respond, a key to helping them stay engaged is to guide them toward serving on a team that is gospel-centered. My grandmother used to say, regarding dating, "You may reach 'em with face powder, but you'll keep 'em with baking powder." In men's ministry, you may attract men with food or an enticing outdoor event, but you will only keep them in the church when the gospel of Jesus Christ invades and transforms the deepest part of their souls. Never change or water down the gospel. Rather, always be willing to change the context in which you give the gospel.

*Transformational Measurement*

Ministry numbers can be a false indicator of health and growth. Church leaders love the energy and support of gathering large numbers of people, for good reason. Each number represents a person, a soul in need of the Savior. Luke recorded in Acts 2:41 that 3,000 people were saved as evidence that God had done a mighty work. Jesus performed a miracle by feeding 5,000 men in Matthew 14:13-21. Local churches have historically used numbers as a measure of success because numbers are easier to quantify than changed lives. But a better tool exists for measuring the health of a church or ministry. Paul taught in 1 Corinthians 6:11(CSB) that transformation is a measurable, visible byproduct of one's conversion experience from nonbeliever to believer:

"But you were washed, you were sanctified, you were justified in the name of the Lord Jesus Christ and by the Spirit of our God."

*Lay-Led Ministry*

Jesus invested His life in a small group of male volunteers who would, in turn, multiply gospel impact globally. This type of miraculous influence only happens through long-term investment and obedience. Perhaps the greatest miracle Jesus ever performed was His ability to gather, unify, train, and launch an eclectic group of men to change the world. Men's ministry leaders will do well to strategically invest in the lives of a few men as Jesus did. This model also shows us that the process of discipleship never ends.

*Discipleship through Multiple Layers of Engagement*

Jesus made disciples through multiple layers of engagement. In John 6, He met the needs of individuals in a large group setting, thereby earning the right to give them the gospel. Mark 10 recorded Jesus calling a small group of ordinary men to abandon all of life's comforts and follow Him as Lord (Mark 10). In Mark 14, Jesus left the larger group of disciples and took His inner circle of three men for deeper investment. In that same chapter, Mark also pointed out the importance of Jesus' personal devotion time with God the Father. This personal and private devotion layer stands as the most critical layer of engagement any person can experience with God.

Large-Group Experience

A great large-group experience presents leaders the opportunity to share big vision. In John 6, Jesus showed the importance of engaging people in a large group. Jesus crossed the Sea of Galilee as a large crowd followed. At this point the people were following Him simply out of a head knowledge of Jesus, the miracle worker. To give them a more intimate experience, he chose to feed 5,000 men, plus women and children, with five loaves of bread and two fish. Jesus knew the crowd was seeking the excitement of the supernatural, but what they really needed to experience was the Savior. Jesus desires that no man be left in his fallen nature. The local church must find ways to engage men, no matter their spiritual condition.

Jesus ministered to the large group, then slipped away with his small group of disciples for debriefing and rest. Jesus did not meet large-group needs just to help the people feel better about their condition. He earned the right to speak truth into the lives of those who would choose to follow Him.

Small-Group Study and Relational Investment

Every man needs at least one 2 a.m. friend, and your wife or mother does not count! Seriously, every man will experience difficulties they will need to talk through; having a trusted, godly friend will prove invaluable. These types of close friendships do not develop easily. They take much time and energy. Many men face the problem of not knowing where or how to develop these types of friendships. What better place than the local church to serve as that place of connection?

Contrary to popular opinion, God creates men to be relational. The world pushes a culture of isolation and teaches men from their early years not to depend on others for fear of disappointment. Consider Peter, Andrew, James, and John, who were fishermen. These disciples were accustomed to spending hours, if not days at a time, alone, and Jesus called them to abandon that lifestyle and follow Him. Perhaps their eagerness to follow Jesus came from an empty well of relational fulfillment? Church leaders should maximize gospel impact as they learn to emphasize ministry with men through large-group experiences *and* small-group investments.

## Daily Private Devotion

The most foundational layer of any disciple-making strategy is one's personal devotion time with God. In Mark 14, Jesus and His disciples were in the Garden of Gethsemane. The master left the disciples and took Peter, James, and John a little farther. After spending some time investing in this even smaller group, Jesus left them to spend time alone with the Father. Why? Jesus loved His disciples, but knew his time to leave the earth was drawing near. The human side of the Savior sought strength, which God provides in an endless supply when we spend regular time with Him.

In Luke 6, Jesus got alone with God and prayed all night. The next morning, He called His followers to Himself and then chose the twelve disciples. The choosing of the twelve disciples is one of the most monumental moments in the Bible, and it is preceded by Jesus' private devotion with the Father. Jesus' private time with God the Father provides two principles for men's ministry: a devotional model to follow and a continual source from which to find strength. Every man needs to spend regular devotional time with God for relational connectedness and supernatural strength.

## A Pipeline of Multiplication

## The Dead Sea Principle

Every Christian man needs at least three types of people in his life: a Paul to serve as a mentor, a "Timothy" in whom to invest, and a Barnabas for encouragement throughout the journey. In this model, a man becomes a disciple, grows as a disciple, and multiplies that experience with other people. Men who live their lives connected in each of these relationships will find the Christian life easier to manage and the gospel impact greater.

It is not enough, however, for men just to find people with whom to share their journey. The Great Commission of our Lord is to "make disciples of all nations." That means we cannot be satisfied with simply soaking up all that the Christian life offers. Every man must learn the Dead Sea principle. The Dead Sea is not dead because it has no fresh water flowing into it. The Dead Sea is dead because it does not have an adequate outlet. We must instill into our men's ministry the God-ordained responsibility that every believer should multiply the gospel seed entrusted to each of us.

Leadership Training

A young preacher once asked me if he should go to seminary or just go straight into the pastorate. I responded, "Both—go to seminary *and* find a way to serve." Seminary education has never been more accessible nor has there ever been a time when it was more needed. False doctrine has invaded the local church as never before, and godly leaders need to stand firm. Leaders must consistently engage in training as they teach the Word of God with integrity and boldness.

Regional events sponsored by your state convention may be an excellent source of training. Many local churches simply cannot afford the overall cost required to host a training event at this level. Leaders can network with other local churches to lighten the burden of expense. Every church would do well to provide money in the annual budget for its leaders to attend some type of regional or national training.

Closed Small Groups

Every man needs an inner circle of men for encouragement and accountability. Many healthy, growing churches have begun what they call Journey Groups. Journey Groups are gender-specific closed groups of three or four people who meet regularly for intense spiritual study, Scripture memory, accountability, and encouragement. These groups do not invite others to join once they begin. They meet for eighteen to twenty-four months and then plan ways in which to multiply.

Jesus had a similar type of small group in Peter, James, and John.

He did things with these men and said things to them that He did not with the other disciples. For more information, check with your state convention representative on how to launch and manage these powerful groups.

Christian Literature

God has gifted many Christians with the ability to write books that instruct, inspire, and encourage. Author Dr. Jay Strack commented, "We have more recorded history in the past 10 years than in the previous history of humanity."[211] If the men in our churches genuinely desire to be agents of change in culture, they must read. Readers are leaders, and leaders must read.

## CONCLUSION

Every church can reach and disciple men in its community. Jesus chose a small group of men to make a global impact as they lived a life that would increasingly resemble Him. These men understood that they were giving their life to something eternal rather than temporal. His disciples were trained to serve locally and were launched to impact the world globally with the gospel of Jesus Christ. Our Lord knew the best way for the gospel to be spread was by His disciples living transformed lives and speaking with boldness. May every church strive to raise up godly men to live with strength and honor in a sin-sick world.

1. What programs need to be laid on the chopping block for your church to better centralize ministry to meet your mission?

2. Does your church culture encourage men to engage in ministry that is God-sized? What must your leadership team do to create this type of vision?

3. Does your church budget reflect the importance of training men to lead?

4. How do you plan to teach men your discipleship strategy and how they can be engaged effectively in ministry?

5. Is your church dependent on a paid professional to do ministry? How can you move toward a healthier leadership model of ministry?

## CHAPTER 15

# MINISTRY LEADERSHIP WITH WOMEN

## Emily Dean

"In the same way, older women are to be reverent in behavior, not slanderers, not slaves to excessive drinking. They are to teach what is good, so they may encourage the young women to love their husbands and to love their children, to be self-controlled, pure, workers at home, kind, and in submission to their husbands, so that God's word will not be slandered."

(Titus 2:3-5 CSB)

Teaching a seminary discipleship class several years ago, my husband polled the group to determine how many students in the class had personally been discipled in a one-on-one setting. Several students raised their hands, and after class, one of the young women with her hand up wanted to know how she could make a connection with an older woman who could disciple her. My husband mentioned the response of the class to me and the specific interest of this student, and I knew then that God was calling me to invest in this young woman. Thus, a relationship was born.

Leading young women in a more formal capacity now, I hear over and over their cries for older women to disciple them. Young women are hungry for the wisdom and guidance of those who are a little further along in the discipleship journey. Why is that? Women crave connection. We see this need throughout Scripture in the relationships of women such as Ruth and Naomi, and Mary and Elizabeth. Women reaching other women is a Biblical concept because God created women with a need for connecting to one another. Think about your own life. How often have you left feeling refreshed after spending time with a spiritually mature woman? Women need other women in their lives who have gone just a little further in their spiritual journeys.

Often, older women are both spiritually mature and physically older. However, sometimes spiritually mature younger women can teach women who are physically older than them. In a mentoring class I taught for ministry wives, one woman in the class chose to mentor her mother because her mother was a new Christian. You may encounter situations where physically older women need to be mentored by more spiritually mature younger women. Likewise, spiritually mature women can disciple other women of similar age in situations where women of their own age are new Christians or have never been discipled. Ideally though, when helping to make connections among women, you will be working to connect physically older and more spiritually mature women to younger women. At any age, God designed women to need each other. The question for ministry leadership with women is how to help women make those connections.

## CONNECTION TRAINING

In my observation, many women know that they should encourage younger women, but they feel ill equipped and insecure about what they would have to offer. Yet younger women just seem to want someone who is a little further along in the journey to befriend them. Young women are eager to be taught, but many older women are hesitant to teach. Our job as ministry leaders is to train and equip the older women to teach the younger women. Training older women to disciple younger women involves the following steps:

*1. Begin with Prayer*

Prayer is absolutely the first step to beginning a ministry of discipling women. God is the one who will give you direction for His plans for the ministry. He will guide you on how to begin and maintain a ministry of discipleship for women. If you do not already have leaders equipped for the ministry, ask Him to bring you two or three ladies with a passion to see women discipled. For each step of the process, continually pray and seek His guidance. Once a ministry is well established, forgetting the step of continual prayer can be easy to do. However, prayer is the most crucial aspect of maintaining any ministry. Pray, pray, and keep praying!

*2. Develop a Vision*

What is your vision for helping women connect in your ministry? When considering vision development for ministry to women, the most important consideration should be what God wants for the ministry. God clearly has a vision for His people. In Acts 1:7, Jesus told the disciples to wait for further direction until the Holy Spirit came. Begin by praying and asking the Lord what He has planned for helping women connect in your ministry.

Every ministry setting is different, so what this ministry looks in your context will be unique to your setting. Before impressing the need upon your women to disciple those younger than them, you will need to develop a clear vision for what this ministry will look like and how you plan to execute your vision. Write down your vision and the specific steps you will need to take to accomplish it.

*3. Help Them See the Need*

To help women connect, older women must first see the need for connection. At one church where my husband and I served, no formal women's ministry was in place when we arrived. I began to talk to women and informally survey the needs in the church. Another woman and I began to pray about where to start. We felt led to begin a women's Bible study. Initially, we thought the group would be comprised of younger stay-at-home moms since we would be meeting during a weekday morning. As the group began, we were surprised to find out that many older and/or retired women wanted to join the group. What a sweet time of fellowship occurred as older women naturally began teaching the younger women through this group!

Often, older women need the connection as much as younger women do, but they must see that younger women truly do want to connect with them. To help them see this need, you will need to communicate your vision for connection to them. After you have developed a clear vision and strategy for ministering to women in your setting, take every opportunity that you have to communicate that vision verbally and through social or print media. Continue to pray and keep the vision before your women. Ask the Lord to provide key women who will encourage other women to be involved. Nothing is more appealing to women than a personal invitation to be involved! As you continue to impress the need upon women to disciple younger women, watch and see as God begins to work in the hearts of women to carry out this biblical directive!

### 4. Help Them Meet the Qualifications

While being a Bible scholar is not required to disciple another woman, growing in spiritual maturity is a necessity. Just before the directive for older women to teach younger women in Titus 2, the apostle Paul outlined spiritual qualifications for older women who teach. Older women should be "reverent in behavior, not slanderers, not slaves to excessive drinking" (Titus 2:3 CSB). Paul did not mean that women should be perfect or spiritual super heroes. What he meant is that women who want to teach others should be growing daily in Christlikeness. Women who are passionately pursuing Christ will have a heart to submit to Him, will be careful to avoid gossiping and criticizing others, and will seek to avoid being controlled by anything other than the Lord Jesus Christ.

If you are serving in a ministry setting in which you find few older ladies who are growing in spiritual maturity, you may need to begin with discipling those ladies first. We must be a disciple before we can make disciples. You might have women who have faithfully attended church their entire lives but who do not know what it truly means to follow wholeheartedly after Jesus. To prepare older women to disciple younger women, you will need to start with where these older ladies are in their spiritual journeys.

One way to help women meet the qualifications for discipling other women is to meet with them for training sessions. These training sessions can be held in a variety of ways according to the needs of your group. You could meet weekly, bi-weekly or monthly for a period of between six weeks to six months. How often your group meets will depend on your setting and what works best for your group. In effect, you would be discipling these ladies to prepare them to disciple others. You may have a few ladies who could help you to train other older women, or you may only have two or three willing to be trained. Start with whom God gives you. Begin to pray that God would raise up and burden the hearts of older ladies to disciple younger ladies.

*5. Help Them Know What to Teach*

A teacher at heart, I love it when God clearly outlines a curriculum! The question of what to teach younger women is very clearly lined out for us in Titus 2. Paul said that the older women are to teach the younger women how to do the following:

1.  Love their husbands
2.  Love their children
3.  Be self-controlled
4.  Be pure
5.  Be homemakers

6. Be kind
7. Be submissive to their husbands

Some women may be hesitant to teach this curriculum because the bookends of this directive are concerning a woman's relationship to her husband. Now clearly, not all women are married and not all women have children. In Paul's day, this would have been a given that most women would be married, yet in 21$^{st}$ century western culture, marriage and children cannot be assumed for women. However, these instructions are applicable to all women because all women can learn to love others. Jesus gave this as the second greatest commandment that we should love our neighbors (Matt. 22:39). To love others, women must submit to the obedience of Christ. While women may or may not have a husband to whom they are called to submit, all Christian women are called to submit to Christ and to submit to one another (Eph. 5:21, 24). In between these bookends, we can see that all women can practice self-control. All women can seek purity. All women can be caretakers of the home God gives them, even if it is a tiny apartment! Most of all, all women can be kind to others.

What God has given to women is a fairly simple curriculum to teach, yet much harder to practice! Often, women are hesitant to teach these things because they feel that they did not carry them out perfectly themselves. Again, what you will want to stress to your older women is that younger women are not looking for someone who has walked the path toward Christlikeness perfectly. In fact, the appearance of perfection is often a turn-off to younger women. What they really desire is to learn from women who are authentic, those who are willing to learn from their mistakes and help others avoid making them.[212] If authentic, spiritually mature women are who younger women are looking for to teach them, so many women in our ministries could apply! To lead women in making connections, we must first develop a vision and strategy to execute that vision, help older women see the need to disciple younger women, help them to meet the qualifications of a spiritually mature woman, and help them know what to teach. Next, we must provide opportunities for women to make connections.

## CONNECTION OPPORTUNITIES

Leading women to disciple other women can happen in a variety of ways. While younger generations tend to want more natural, organic approaches than the preference of older generations for formal organization[213], some structure will be necessary to help women connect. While natural connections may be preferred, without some structure connections often fail to happen. The biggest issue I hear from younger women is that they want older women to disciple them, but they do not know how to go about finding them. What I encourage them to do is to put themselves in opportunities where they will naturally be able to meet older women. Depending on your ministry context, women may want to connect through small groups, events, or one-on-one mentoring.

Small groups are a means for helping women connect that can be formal or informal. The time and length the group meets as well as the depth of topic can be varied and will depend on the needs of your group. Often, these groups tend to develop with women of similar ages or in a similar life stage, such as young moms, widows, etc. Groups can be specific to Bible study, prayer, special interest, or strategic support.[214] However, as I mentioned before with the group I experienced, sometimes women from multiple generations will come together to create a group. To intentionally involve women across different age groups, you will need to communicate that you desire the groups to be inter-generational. You may have enough women to start with one group, or you may be able to create multiple groups. Prior to starting your group, you can begin the step of training your older women to be intentional about connecting with younger women in the group. If older women clearly see their purpose in the group is to disciple the younger women, then they will more likely be intentional about investing in the younger women.

Events are a natural means for women to meet other women that they would not likely meet otherwise. As mentioned before, younger women prefer natural connections to anything that appears to be formal or programmatic. However, events are a path for women to create natural connections. I often educate younger women on the need to attend events so that they can make the natural connections for which they are looking. You do not have to provide a large formal event unless that is what your women desire. Even casual events such as an informal coffee or movie/craft night can provide the opportunity for women to meet one another. Younger women should not sit idly by waiting for older women to connect with them. They have a responsibility as well to attend events where they can get to know other women.

Retreats are a longer type of event that typically last one or two nights. However, retreats can also be a one day event on your ministry site or at a different location. The purpose of a retreat is connecting with other women and spiritual growth.[215] Retreats planned for the purpose of helping women make connections can be a great opportunity for women to get to know one another in greater depth than a two or three-hour event can provide.

Small groups, events, or retreats can be your main focus for connecting women. However, if women desire to connect through one-on-one relationships, they can also be your launching point for connecting women in discipling relationships. Women are often busy and hesitant to agree to an intense weekly commitment.[216] For one-to-one discipling relationships to work, what must be communicated to both older and younger women is that flexibility is key. The time and length of commitment will depend on the individual women involved.

One-to-one mentoring in my life has been experienced through what I like to call "mentoring on the go." I have learned individually from women as we have served together in a variety of ministry roles. I have watched and observed. I have asked questions about how they handle situations. I have learned from them as we have served together. While I am still learning from many women, I am also teaching other young women as I go and as we serve together. If the women in your ministry setting do not feel like they have the time to meet regularly in a one-on-one setting, then perhaps you could rethink your model for helping women connect. Help them to find ways to serve together and learn from one another.

## CONNECTION SUPPORT

In addition to providing training opportunities, women serving in leadership roles need on-going support to continue in their roles of mentoring women. First, women need encouragement! Investing yourself into the life of another person can be exhausting and emotionally and spiritually draining, which is why so many women give up after a short time of mentoring. You, as the women's ministry leader or discipleship leader, have the opportunity to continually cheer on the ladies serving in your ministry to women. You can remind them through text or social media verses of encouragement, such as Galatians 6:9, "Let us not get tired of doing good, for we will reap at the proper time if we don't give up" (CSB). Let them know that their service to the Lord is important, and that it is making a kingdom difference, even if they cannot see immediate fruit. Be their constant source of encouragement!

Next, women need clear expectations. In addition to discussing qualifications for service, women need to know what is expected of them and what support they can expect from their leader. Regarding the mentoring relationships, women often develop a written covenant for both the mentor and mentee. While written agreements formalize the mentoring process, they also provide accountability for the women involved in the mentoring relationship.

Women serving other women also need resources to help them with unfamiliar situations. Thankfully, we live in an era in which an abundance of resources exists for training in ministry to women. Formal options, such as seminary classes, workshops, and training conferences are available in addition to informal print or online media. Search out resources to continually give your ladies who are in leadership training tips and information that would be helpful to them as they mentor other women. You may even want to go through a book together or attend a conference as a leadership team. Finally, ask the women with whom you are serving what resources they need to assist them in your ministry to women.

Assistance with counseling and referral is another area of support needed in ministry to women. In mentoring women, delicate information may often be shared. The mentor may find herself in a situation for which she feels ill equipped and unprepared to handle. Women's ministry leaders need to know that it is okay to admit when counsel is required beyond their capabilities of helping. In those circumstances that are beyond basic counseling needs, she may need to refer the mentee to a professional counselor. Women's ministry leaders need information about where to refer women in situations when professional help is needed.

Finally, an ongoing evaluation of the ministry is important to help new and existing mentoring relationships develop and thrive. Leaders must be able to share both positive and negative aspects of the ministry, and mentees also need the opportunity to share what they need and would like to see included in the ministry of mentoring. Providing opportunities for evaluation of the ministry will allow the ministry to adjust as needed to maintain and promote further growth.

As you seek the Lord concerning what ministry leadership with women should look like in your church setting, here are some questions to consider:

## CONNECTION POINTS

1. Whom do you have praying with you about your ministry to women? If none beyond yourself, write down the names of two or three ladies you would like to enlist to begin praying with you.

2. What is the vision for your ministry to women? Take a few minutes to write out your vision/purpose statement.

3. What opportunities for training will you provide to equip your leaders?

4. What would be the most effective means in your setting to provide natural opportunities for women to connect? (i.e. one-to-one, small groups, events)

5. In what ways can you support your leaders in ministry to women?

## AFTERWORD

We have been honored to facilitate a guide to the two driving concepts in ministry that parallel our equipping the people of the church to do the work: discipleship and ministry leadership. Several hundred years of ministry experience, combined with research in the various aspects of discipleship and ministry leadership have arrived at the conclusion of their contributed chapter with reflections and questions for you to process and consider for your ministry. We intentionally did not provide you a step-by-step guide or a model of how to implement all the chapters as one total equipping strategy. Each chapter was intentionally crafted to flow into the next, but with the ability to skip chapters and read them in the order you desire. As editors, we believed the foundation was crucial and that each chapter that followed in the discipleship section provided a great progression to what should happen each week in the church. We then consulted colleagues that are working each week in the area of ministry leadership that their chapter unpacked.

They have provided you with a snapshot of what each of those seven crucial components of lifespan ministry with children through senior adults for discipleship to be a part of ministry leadership. We could have written more chapters but we have realized that most churches are stretched to have ministry leadership with a staff person or through a team to cover these seven areas. The landscape of small, medium, and large churches can all benefit from what is written. Do not be discouraged if you cannot address everything in the next few months for discipleship and ministry leadership. Begin to craft a plan for what you can do effectively and work toward creating a culture in your church where discipleship is a priority. The ministry leadership should have ways to be equipped to disciple each age group and be sure that an area of the lifespan is not missing if possible in your context. We understand that some churches are missing some age groups and we pray that as you focus on discipleship that churches would be healthy and intergenerational. If you desire to continue to receive information we have a center for Discipleship and Ministry Leadership to help you that can be followed on Twitter, liked on Facebook, or visited at www.nobts.edu. The center also sponsors conferences and can provide training for you at your church. We call these Xcelerate events which occur on the main campus and can be taken on the road to where you serve. Contact us if we can help you with your ministry.

# ABOUT THE CONTRIBUTORS

Hal Stewart

Hal is the Associate Professor of Discipleship, Director of Spiritual Formation and Director of the Doctor of Education Degree Program at New Orleans Baptist Theological Seminary. Prior to his teaching at NOBTS, Stewart served for 13 years in church ministry roles overseas in Kenya and South Carolina, Mississippi, and Tennessee. He is married to Julie Moore Stewart and they are blessed with three children: Trey, Jordan, and Hallie. He earned his Ph.D. and Th.M. (New Orleans Baptist Theological Seminary), MDiv (Southeaster Baptist Theological Seminary), Master of Education and Bachelor of Science (Clemson University).

Scott Jones

Scott is Assistant Dean of Discipleship & Christian Formation and Professor of Christian Ministry at Bryan College in Dayton, TN. Prior to his service at Bryan College, Jones served for 16 years in various local church pastoral roles in Mississippi and Louisiana. In addition to his current service at Bryan College, Jones serves local churches through pulpit supply and consultation. He is married to Kimberly Meador Jones, and they are blessed with twins who are seniors in college: Hannah Paige and Seth Thomas. He earned a PhD (New Orleans Baptist Theological Seminary, 2005) and DMin (Reformed Theological Seminary, 1999).

David Evans

David is a surrendered follower of Jesus. He is married to Stephanie and they have two children (10) Emma and Jackson (5). He planted and pastored Epiphany Baptist Church in Springfield for 16 years and is currently the Evangelism Team Leader for the Tennessee Baptist Mission Board. He is a graduate of The Southern Baptist Theological Seminary (M.Div and Th.M) and the New Orleans Baptist Theological Seminary (Th.M and Ph.D.).

Jody Dean

Jody is Assistant Professor of Christian Education, Senior Regional Associate Dean for LA/MS Extension Centers, and Director of Mentoring Programs in Christian Education at New Orleans Baptist Theological Seminary. He has a passion for developing disciples and ministry leaders for the church. He is married to Emily and they have two children Lydia (10) and James Robert (5). He is a graduate of Leavell College (BA), and New Orleans Baptist Theological Seminary (M.Div, Th.M, and Ph. D.).

Eddie Mosley

Eddie has served as Small Groups Pastor at LifePoint Church, a multi-site campus in Smyrna, TN, since 2005. His enthusiasm for seeing life change happen in the lives of individuals in his church, neighborhood and community is infectious. Eddie is author of *Connecting in Communities, Understanding the Dynamics of Small Groups* and various other articles on practical approaches to reaching people for Bible study. He is a sought after speaker for small group ministry as well as neighborhood impact. His passion is to help pastors and leaders develop a strategy to implement Small Groups that build community and impact their communities. He complete an M.Div degree at The Southern Baptist Theological Seminary and a D.Min degree at the New Orleans Baptist Theological Seminary.

David Bond

David has served on the staff of the Arkansas Baptist State Convention on the Evangelism and Church Health Team and the Executive Team, since 2009. His focus areas are in Church Revitalization, adult Sunday School/Small Group ministries and Christian higher education. A native of Houston, Texas, David grew up in Ashdown, AR, and is a graduate of Ouachita Baptist University (BME), Southwestern Baptist Theological Seminary (MACE), and New Orleans Baptist Theological Seminary (ThM, PhD). Prior to joining the ABSC staff, David served churches in Arkansas and Nashville, TN, as a minister of youth/music, minister of education, and pastor. David and his wife, Renee, are the parents of two daughters.

Adam Hughes

Adam serves as the Dean of Chapel, Director of the Adrian Rogers Center for Expository Preaching, Director of the Mentoring Programs in Pastoral Ministries, and Assistant Professor of Expository Preaching at New Orleans Baptist Theological Seminary. Having over 15 years of experiences in the local church, he now teaches courses in preaching, leadership, and pastoral ministries. Adam has been a guest speaker and lecturer for convention sermons, chapel services, expository preaching workshops, and multiply revivals. He and his wife Holly have four children and live in New Orleans. He is a graduate of the University of Arkansas at Little Rock (BA) and Southwestern Baptist Theological Seminary (MDiv and Ph.D.)

Randy Stone

Randy is Professor of Christian Education, Chair, Discipleship and Ministry Leadership Division, and Director of the Doctor of Educational Ministry at New Orleans Baptist Theological Seminary. Before joining the faculty, Randy held multiple staff positions at churches in Louisiana, Missouri, North Carolina and Texas. He also taught at Southwestern Baptist Theological Seminary and Liberty University Online Seminary. Randy enjoys church consulting and regularly leads ministry leadership conferences and workshops. He serves on the Board of the Baptist Association of Christian Educators (BACE) and is a member of the Society of Professors of Christian Education (SPCE). Randy earned the M.R.E. from Midwestern Baptist Theological Seminary, and ThM and PhD in Christian Education from New Orleans Baptist Theological Seminary.

## Faye Scott

Faye serves as the Minister to Children at First Baptist New Orleans. She has served in children's ministry for over twenty years. Faye is currently pursuing a Doctor of Education Degree at New Orleans Baptist Theological Seminary. She leads training events for preschool and children's ministry workers and leaders throughout the Southern Region of the United States. She also serves as adjunct faculty for Leavell College of New Orleans Baptist Theological Seminary. Her greatest joy is the time she spends with her three children and six grandchildren.

## Jonathan Denton

Jonathan has served in youth ministry for almost twenty years. He is currently an Assistant Professor of Christian Studies at Charleston Southern University. He is married to Amanda and has two young boys, Josiah (6) and Baxter (3). He earned his Master of Divinity, Master of Theology, and Doctor of Philosophy degrees from New Orleans Baptist Theological Seminary.

## David Odom

David is Associate Professor of Student Ministry at New Orleans Baptist Theological Seminary and serves as the Director of the Youth Ministry Institute. He holds a B.A. from Liberty University along with an MARE and Ph.D. from Southwestern Baptist Theological Seminary. Before joining the faculty at NOBTS, Dr. Odom served as Youth Minister in churches in Texas and Alabama. He has a heart for teenagers and emerging adults and loves finding creative ways to disciple young people. Dr. Odom has been married to his wife, Natalie, for twenty-seven years. They have two teenage daughters and live in Covington, LA.

Bert Ross

Bert has over 40 years' serving as leader in Church and Denominational ministry. He is a Certified Executive Coach and holds a Professional Certification in Human Resource Management with the Society of Human Resource Management. He serves as a trainer/facilitator in leadership and organizational development in ministry and corporate settings. Bert graduated from Columbia Int. University with a B.S. in Education and has a Master's degree in Leadership Development and Organizational Leadership from Trinity Bible College and Seminary and a Master's Degree in Human Resource Development from Clemson University. He is currently working on his D.Ed.Min at Orleans Theological Seminary.

Loretta Rivers

Loretta is Professor of Social Work at New Orleans Baptist Theological Seminary. Her teaching interests include gerontology, church and community ministries, and social work. She enjoys teaching Bible fellowship classes for homebound adults and women 65+ at First Baptist Covington, LA. She is a graduate of New Orleans Baptist Theological Seminary (MACE), Louisiana State University (MSW), and Tulane University (Ph.D).

Scott Sullivan

Scott is married to the love of his life, Elizabeth. They have four children: Erika, Austin, Caleb, and Noah. He serves as equipping pastor at First Baptist Haughton, La. Scott is an author, discipleship consultant, disciple-maker, and speaker. He is passionate about Jesus, family, and the outdoors. He earned his Doctor of Education Ministry degree from New Orleans Baptist Theological Seminary.

Emily Dean

Emily serves as Adjunct Professor and Director of Women's Academic Programs and Organizations at New Orleans Baptist Theological Seminary. She and her husband Jody, along with their two children Lydia and James Robert, live in New Orleans where Jody serves as assistant professor of Christian Education at NOBTS. Passionate about training and equipping women, Emily currently teaches at NOBTS in the Women's Ministry and Ministry Wife Programs. She earned her Master of Divinity, Master of Theology, and her Doctor of Philosophy degrees from New Orleans Baptist Theological Seminary.

# NOTES

## Chapter 1:

1   All Scripture references from the Bible for all chapters of this book are from the Christian Standard Bible.

2   Keith Krell, "Grace to the End: Part 10, https://bible.org/seriespage/10-grace-end-1-thessalonians-523-28#P860_309202, accessed 10 July 2017.

3   Greg Ogden, Transforming Discipleship, 39.

4   Dallas Willard, *The Great Omission: Reclaiming Jesus' Essential Teaching on Discipleship* (San Francisco, CA: Harper Collins, 2006), 53.

5   John Piper. "God is Most Glorified in Us When We Are Most Satisfied in Him," In The Christian Educator's Handbook on Spiritual Formation, eds. Kenneth Gangel and James C. Wilhoit (1992, Baker Books: Grand Rapids, MI.), 74-85..

6   John M. Dettoni, "What is Spiritual Formation." In The Christian Educator's Handbook on Spiritual Formation, eds. Kenneth Gangel and James C. Wilhoit (1992, Baker Books: Grand Rapids, MI.), 15.

7   A.W. Tozer, *The Knowledge of the Holy* (New York: HarperCollins, 1961), 1.

8   Dallas Willard and Jan Johnson, *Renovation of the Heart in Daily Practice: Experiments in Spiritual Transformation* (Colorado Springs: CO: NavPress, 2006), 72.

9   W.E. Vine, "Epignosis," in Vine's Expository Dictionary of Old and New Testament Words (Old Tappan, NJ: Revell, 1981), 301.

10   Stanley J. Grenz, *The Social God and the Relational Self: A Trinitarian theology of the Imago Dei* (Louisville, KY: Westminster John Knox Press, 2001), 5.

11   Diane Chandler, *Christian Spiritual Formation: An Integrated Approach for Personal and Relational Wholeness* (Downers Grove, IL: Intervarsity Press, 2014), 123.

12   Rick Melick and Shera Melick, *Teaching That Transforms: Facilitating Life Change Through Adult Bible Teaching* (Nashville, TN: Broadman and Holman, 2010), 86.

13   Henry Holloman, *The Forgotten Blessing* (Nashville, TN: Word Publishing, 1999), 6.

14  John Ortberg, The Life You've Always Wanted: Spiritual Disciplines for Ordinary People (Grand Rapids, MI: Zondervan, 2002), 45-6.

15  Robert W. Pazmino, *God Our Teacher: Theological Basics in Christian Education*, (Grand Rapids, MI: Baker Academic, 2001), 9-10.

16  Robert W. Pazmino, *Foundational Issues in Christian Education* (Grand Rapids, MI:Baker Books, 1997), 191.

17  John R. Tyson, ed. *Invitation to Christian Spirituality: An Ecumenical Anthology* (New York, NY: Oxford University Press, 1999), 3.

## Chapter 2:

18  Ed Stetzer, *Exegete Your Culture: 10 Checkpoints for Knowing and Reaching Your Culture* (Ed Stetzer & Mission Group, 2016), 4.

19  Paul B. Hiebert, *Anthropological Insights for Missionaries* (Grand Rapids: Baker, 1985), 30.

20  Geert Hofstede, *Cultures and Organizations: Software of the Mind* (New York: McGraw Hill, 1997), 5.

21  Seth Godin, *Tribes: We Need You to Lead Us* (New York: Penguin Group, 2008), 1-2.

22  Duane Elmer, *Cross-Cultural Servanthood: Serving the World in Christlike Humility* (Downers Grove, IL: 2006), 125.

23  Elmer, 136.

24  A Scott Moreau, Gary R. Corwin, and Gary B. McGee, *Introducing World Missions: A Biblical, Historical and Practical Survey, 2nd ed.* (Grand Rapids: Baker Academic, 2015), 16.

25  David A. Livermore, *Cultural Intelligence: Improving Your CQ to Engage Our Multicultural World* (Grand Rapids: Baker Academic, 2009), 13.

26  Ibid, 14, 85.

27  Ibid., 14, 180; and Stetzer, 23.

28  Livermore, 213; and Elmer, 126.

29  Livermore, 233, 123-39; Moreau, Corwin, and McGee, 255-61.

30  Stetzer, 5-8.

31  Ibid., 14.

32  Ibid., 19.

33  Erich Baumgartner, "The Impact of Cultural Factors on Leadership in a Global Church," Journal of Adventist Mission Studies 7, no. 1 (2011): 56.

34  David Kinnaman and Gabe Lyons, *Good Faith: Being a Christian When Society Thinks You're Irrelevant and Extreme* (Grand Rapids: Baker Books, 2016), 54-7.

35  The New Moral Code and all of the related statistics can be found in Kinnaman and Lyons, 57; and Roxanne Stone, ed., *Barna Trends 2017* (Grand Rapids, MI: Baker, 2016), 50-3, 178.

36   A comprehensive description of these two groups of statistics can be found in David Kinnaman and Gabe Lyons, *Unchristian: What a New Generation Really Thinks About Christianity...And Why It Matters* (Grand Rapids, MI: Baker Books, 2007) and David Kinnaman, *You Lost Me: Why Young Christians are Leaving Church...and Rethinking Faith (Grand Rapids, MI: Baker Books, 2011)*.

37   Kinnaman and Lyons, *Good Faith*, 12.

38   David Platt, *Counter Culture: Following Christ in an Anti-Christian Age*, rev. ed. (Carol Stream, IL: Tyndale House Publishers, 2017), 1.

39   Kinnaman and Lyons, *Good Faith*, 248.

40   Platt, xv and remainder of book.

41   Kinnaman and Lyons, *Good Faith*, 201.

42   Stone, 134-5, 195.

43   Baumgartner, 57-8.

44   GLOBE stands for Global Leadership and Organizational Behavior Effectiveness; these and other results of this study can be found in R. J. House et al., *Culture, Leadership, and Organizations: The GLOBE Study of 62 Societies* (Thousand Oaks, CA: Sage, 2004).

45   Stetzer, 10-1.

## Chapter 3:

46   Lewis Drummond, *The Word of the Cross: A Contemporary Theology of Evangelism* (Nashville, TN: Broadman and Holman, 1992), 188.

47   A definition provided by the Google Search Engine when searching for "assumption definition."

48   Francis Chan and Danae Yankoski, *Forgotten God: Reversing Our Tragic Neglect of the Holy Spirit* (Colorado Springs, CO: David C. Cook, 2009), 31.

49   John MacArthur, *Hard to Believe: The High Cost and Infinite Value of Following Jesus* (Nashville, TN: Thomas Nelson Publishers, 2003), 188.

50   Refer to Ed Stetzer, "No Such Thing as 'The Gift of Evangelism,'" http://www.christianitytoday.com/edstetzer/2010/july/no-such-thing-as-gift-of-evangelism.html (accessed July 11, 2017).

51   Refer to Thom Rainer, *Effective Evangelistic Churches: Successful Churches Reveal What Works and What Doesn't* (Nashville, TN: Broadman and Holman, 1996), 13.

52   Robert Coleman, *The Master Plan of Evangelism* (Grand Rapids, MI: Revell, 1994), 11-2.

53   J. I. Packer, *Evangelism and the Sovereignty of God* (Downers Grove, IL: InterVarsity Press, 1991), 87.

54   William R. Estep, *Whole Gospel Whole World: The Foreign Mission Board of the Southern Baptist Convention 1845-1995* (Nashville, TN: Broadman and Holman Publishers, 1994), 148.

55   A. W. Tozer, *Of God and Men* (Chicago, IL: Moody Publishers, 1988), 15.

56   Refer to Steve Sjogren, *Conspiracy of Kindness: A Refreshing New Approach to Sharing the Love of Jesus* (Grand Rapids, MI: Baker Publishing Group, 2003); and Alvin Reid, *Sharing Jesus Without Freaking Out: Evangelism the Way You Were Born To Do It* (Nashville, TN: Broadman and Holman Publishers, 2017).

57   Russell Moore, *Onward: Engaging the Culture Without Losing the Gospel* (Nashville, TN: Broadman and Holman, 2015), 109.

58   A statement made to the author.

59   Chuck Kelley, "The New Methodists," http://www.drchuckkelley.com/2014/04/08/the-new-methodists-part-two/ (accessed July 11, 2017).

60   Refer to Alvin Reid, *Evangelism Handbook: Biblical, Spiritual, Intentional, Missional* (Nashville, TN: Broadman and Holman Publishers, 2009), 165.

## Chapter 4:

61   Bobb Biehl, *Mentoring: Confidence in Finding a Mentor and Becoming One* (Nashville, TN: Broadman and Holman Publishers, 1996), 19.

62   Todd Wilson, *More* (Grand Rapids, MI: Zondervan, 2016), 196.

63   Andy Stanley and Bob Willits, *Creating Community: 5 Keys to Building a Small Group Culture* (Colorado Springs, CO: Multnomah, 2004), 22.

64   Deitrich Bonhoeffer, *The Cost of Discipleship* (New York, NY: Touchstone, 1959), 94

## Chapter 5:

65   Margaret Mead, "Margaret Mead Quotes," Brainyquote.com, accessed July 15, 2017, https://www.brainyquote.com/quotes/authors/m/margaret_mead.html.

66   Christian Standard Bible

67   Myers, Joseph R, *The Search to Belong, Rethinking Intimacy, Community, and Small Groups* (Grand Rapids: Zondervan, 2003), 142.

68   Steve Gladen, *Small Groups with Purpose, How to Create Healthy Communities* (Grand Rapids, MI: Baker Books, 2011), 132.

69   Eddie Mosley, *Connecting in Communities, Understanding the Dynamics of Small Groups* (Colorado Springs, CO: NavPress, 2011), 119-20.

## Chapter 6:

70   "Davenport doorman honored for 75 years of service", The Spokesman-Review, Abby Lynes, June 1, 2017. Available at http://www.spokesman.com/stories/2017/jun/01/davenport-doorman-honored-for-75-years-of-service/#/0 (accessed July 15, 2017).

71  "Reasons Adults Switch Churches", LifeWay Research, March 30, 2007, available at http://lifewayresearch.com/2007/03/30/reasons-adults-switch-churches/ (accessed July 1, 2017).

72  Kevin Ford, *Transforming Church* (Carol Stream, IL: Tyndale House, 2007), 12.

73  "Selflessness Leads to Spiritual Maturity", LifeWay Research, November 19, 2012, available at http://lifewayresearch.com/2012/11/19/selflessness-leads-to-spiritual-maturity/ (accessed July 8, 2017).

74  "Post-flood ministry yields church's wave of baptisms." Brian Blackwell, Baptist Press, February 24, 2017, available at http://www.bpnews.net/48404/postflood-ministry-yields-churchs-wave-of-baptisms (accessed July 8, 2017).

75  Mark Clifton, *Reclaiming Glory* (Nashville, TN: Broadman and Holman, 2016), 67.

76  Eric Geiger and Kevin Peck, *Designed to Lead* (Nashville, TN: Broadman and Holman, 2016), 153.

77  Clifton, 63.

78  Jim Putman, *Church is a Team Sport* (Grand Rapids, MI: Baker Books, 2008), 125.

79  Ed Stetzer, Richie Stanley, and Jason Hayes, *Lost and Found* (Nashville, TN: Broadman and Holman, 2009), 155-56.

80  Alvin Reid and David Wheeler, *Servanthood Evangelism*, (Gospel Advance Books, 2013), 22.

81  Jason K. Allen, *Discerning Your Call to Ministry* (Chicago, IL: Moody, 2016), 19-20.

## Chapter 7:

82  Jim Shaddix, "Pulpit Discipleship: Shepherding People to Christlikeness Through Preaching," in *Progress in the Pulpit: How to Grow in Your Preaching* (Chicago: Moody, 2017), 62.

83  David Schrok, "What has preaching to do with discipleship?" in *Essential Reading on Preaching* (Louisville: Southern Equip, 2017), 59.

84  Shaddix, "Pulpit Discipleship," 62.

85  Unless otherwise noted, all Scripture quotation are from the New American Standard Bible, 2002.

86  John B. Polhill, *Acts,* The New American Commentary, vol. 26 (Nashville: Broadman Press, 1992), 273.

87  Ibid.

88  Shaddix, "Pulpit Discipleship," 62.

89  Mark Dever and Greg Gilbert, *Preach: Theology Meets Practice* (Nashville: B&H, 2012), 48.

90  Mark Dever, *Discipling: How to Help Others Follow Jesus* (Wheaton: Crossway, 2016), 60.

91  Ibid., 38.

92  Dever and Gilbert, *Preach*, 36.

93  Shaddix, "Pulpit Discipleship," 73–74.

94  Dever, *Discipling*, 38. Italics mine for emphasis.

95  GregOgden, *Transforming Discipleship: Making Disciples a Few at a Time* (Downers Grove: InterVarsity Press, 2003), 163.

96  Francis Chan, *Multiple: Disciples Making Disciples* (Colorado Springs: David C. Cook, 2012), 91.

97  Dever and Gilbert, *Preach*, 57.

98  Ibid., 52.

99  Aubrey Malphurs, *Being Leaders: The Nature of Authentic Christian Leadership* (Grand Rapids: Baker, 2003), 10.

100 R. Bruce Bickel, *Light and Heat: The Puritan View of the Pulpit* (Morgan, PA: Soli Deo Gloria, 1999), 73.

101 James Emory White, "Preaching and Administration" in *Handbook of Contemporary Preaching: A Wealth of Counsel for Creative and Effective Proclamation*, ed. Michael Duduit (Nashville: Broadman and Holman, 1992), 461.

102 Shaddix, "Pulpit Discipleship," 65.

## For Further Reading:

Crites, Tom and Steve Parr. *Why They Stay: Helping Parents and Church Leaders Make Investments That Keep Children and Teens Connected to the Church for a Lifetime.* Bloomington, IN: WestBow Press, 2015.

Elmore, Tim. *Generation iY: Secrets to Connecting with Today's Teens and Young Adults in the Digital Age.* Atlanta, GA: Poet Gardner Publishing, 2015.

Everts, Don and Doug Schaupp. *I Once Was Lost: What Postmodern Skeptics Taught Us About Their Path to Jesus.* Downers Grove, IL: InterVarsity Press, 2008.

Kinnaman, David. *Unchristian: What a New Generation Really Thinks about Christianity ... and Why It Matters.* Grand Rapids, MI: Baker Books, 2007.

Kramp, John. *Out of Their Faces and Into Their Shoes: How to Understand Spiritually Lost People and Give Them Directions to God.* Nashville, TN: Broadman and Holman Publishers, 1995.

Pippert, Rebecca Manley. *Out of the Salt Shaker and Into the World: Evangelism as a Way of Life.* Downers Grove, IL: InterVarsity Press, 1999.

Ritzer, George. *The McDonaldization of Society 6.* Thousand Oaks, CA: SAGE Publications, 2011.

## Chapter 8:

103 http://www.history.com/topics/american-revolution/battles-of-trenton-and-princeton.

104 https://www.youtube.com/watch?v=TrJJ6ncp1fc.

105  Gen 1:26-27, 2:7, CSB.

106  Gen 2:15-17, CSB.

107  Gal 4:4, CSB.

108  John 6:35-40, CSB.

109  John 10:17-18, CSB.

110  John 17:3-4, CSB.

111  Henry Blackaby. *Spiritual Leadership*. Nashville, TN: Broadman and Holman Publishers, 2001. 87

112  Numbers 12:3, CSB.

113  Psalm 149:4, CSB.

114  Phil 2:8, CSB.

115  Matt 18:4, CSB, Luke 14: 11, CSB.

116  Romans 5:1, CSB, Romans 3:22, CSB.

117  Romans 14:23, CSB.

118  Hebrews 11:1, CSB.

119  Hebrews 11:6, CSB.

120  Joseph Stowell. *Redefining Leadership*. Grand Rapids, MI: Zondervan. 2014., 25.

121  Blackaby 127.

122  http://www.sbpcshape.org/.

123  Ted Engstrom *The Making of a Christian Leader*. Grand Rapids, MI: Zondervan. 1976. 90.

124  Malphurs, Aubrey *Being Leaders*. Grand Rapids, MI: Baker Publishing. 2001, Appdendix K. 201.

## Chapter 9:

125  http://www.smh.com.au/news/big-questions/why-do-buildings-need-founda tions/2008/05/28/1211654096508.html; Why do Buildings Need Foundations, Harriet Veith, May 24, 2008; accessed June 17, 2017.

126  https://www.merriam-webster.com/dictionary/foundation; accessed June 17, 2017.

127  http://www.coastalbridge.com/deep-foundation-and-pile-driving-construction-explained/

128  Make it Righthttp://makeitright.org/what-we-know/library/article/foundation/; accessed June 17, 2017.

129  https://theconstructor.org/geotechnical/foundation-types-and-uses/9237/ Types of Foundations for Buildings and their Uses in Construction; accessed July 1, 2017. pes

130  Matthew 7:25b, CSB.

131  Steve Adams, *Children's Ministry on Purpose: A Purpose Driven Approach to Lead Kids Toward Spiritual Health* (Grand Rapids, MI: Zondervan, 2017), 99-100.

132  Jana Magruder, *Kids Ministry That Nourishes: Three Essentials of a Healthy Kids Ministry* (Nashville: B & H Publishing Group, 2016), 56.

133  Levels of Biblical Learning

134  https://www.simplypsychology.org/Erik-Erikson.html; accessed July 1, 2017. Erik Erickson, Saul McLeod, published 2008, updated 2017.

135  http://biblehub.com/commentaries/psalms/78-72.htm. Pulpit Commentary.

136  Matthew Poole's Commentary, http://biblehub.com/commentaries/psalms/78-72.htm

## Chapter 10:

137  Dr. Jackson has a great book on discipleship of students that goes into a lot more detail than I can in a chapter. Allen Jackson, Disciple: The Ordinary Person's Guide to Discipling Teenagers (youthministry360, 2015).

138  Chap Clark, *Hurt: inside the world of today's teenagers* (Grand Rapids, MI: Baker Academic, 2004), 55-56.

139  Kara Powell, Jake Mulder, and Brad Griffin. *Growing Young: Six essential strategies to help young people discover and love your church* (Grand Rapids: Baker Books, 2016), 166-168.

140  Thom S. Rainer and Eric Geiger. *Simple Church* (Nashville: B&H Publishing Group, 2006), 115.

141  Here is a link from Cru of a great article on finding the right people for discipleship https://www.cru.org/content/dam/cru/legacy/2012/01/therightpeople.pdf.

142  Jimmie Davis, *Girls Ministry Handbook* (Nashville: LifeWay Press, 2007).

143  Richard Ross, *Student Ministry and the Supremacy of Christ* (Bloomington, IN: CrossBooks, 2009), 39.

## Chapter 11:

144  Christian Smith, *Lost in Transition: The Dark Side of Emerging Adulthood* (New York, NY: Oxford University Press, 2011), 226.

145  Jean Piaget, "Intellectual evolution from adolescent to adulthood" in Human Development, vol. 51 (2008), 42.

146  Eric Erikson, *Childhood and Society, 2nd Edition* (New York, NY: Horton, 1963), 263.

147  Sharan B. Merriam and Ralph G. Brockett, *The Profession and Practice of Adult Education: An Introduction* (San Francisco, CA: Jossey-Bass, 2007), 8.

148  Margaret Lawson, "The Adult Learner," in *The Teaching Ministry of the Church 2nd Edition* (Nashville, TN: B&H Academic, 2009), 351.

149  Jeffrey Jensen Arnett, *Emerging Adulthood: The Winding Road from the Late Teens through the Twenties,* 2nd Edition (New York: Oxford University Press, 2014), 15.

150  Ibid, 7.

151  Richard Ross, *Accelerate: Parenting teenagers toward adulthood* (Bloomington, IN: CrossBooks, 2013), 2.

152  Arnett, 4.

153  Ibid.

154  Ross, 2.

155  Smith, *Lost in Transition*,13-14.

156  Ross, 3.

157  Tim Elmore, *Generation iY* (Atlanta, GA: Poet Gardner, 2010), 94.

158  Ross, 3.

159  David P. Setran and Chris A. Kiesling, *Spiritual Formation in Emerging Adulthood: A practical theology for college and young adult ministry* (Grand Rapids, MI: Baker Academic, 2013), 62.

160  Sparks & Honey, "Meet Generation Z: Forget Everything You Learned About Millennials," LinkedIn SlideShare. N.p., 17 June 2014. Accessed October 14, 2017.

161  Corey Seemiller and Meghan Grace, *Generation Z Goes to College* (San Francisco, CA: Jossey-Bass, 2016), 27.

162  Tim Elmore, *Marching off the Map* (Atlanta, GA: Poet Gardner, 2017), Kindle.

163  Christian Smith and Melinda Denton, *Soul Searching: The Religious and Spiritual Lives of American Teenagers* (New York, NY: Oxford University Press, 2005), 162.

164  Ross, 4.

165  David Kinnaman, *You Lost Me: Why Young Christians are Leaving the Church . . . and Rethinking Faith* (Grand Rapids, MI: Baker Books, 2011), 28.

166  Ibid, 22.

167  Ibid, 25.

168  Steve Parr and Tom Crites, *Why They Stray: Helping Parents and Church Leaders Make Investments That Keep Children and Teens Connected to the Church for a Lifetime* (Bloomington, IN: WestBow Press, 2015), 120.

169  Ibid, 121.

170  Setran and Kiesling, 62.

171  Thomas Bergler, *The Juvenilization of American Christianity* (Grand Rapids, MI: Eerdmans, 2012), 2.

172  Parr and Crites, 122.

173  Kinnaman, 28.

174  Greg Ogden, *Transforming Discipleship* (Downers Grove, IL: InterVarsity Press, 2003), 121.

175  175 Kinnaman, 206.

176  Frank Dennis, *Reaching Single Adults* (Grand Rapids, MI: Baker Publishing Group, 2007), 50.

177  Josh Packard, *Church Refugees* (Loveland, CO: Group Publishing, 2015), 50.

178 Sharon Galgay Ketcham, "Faith Formation with Others," in *Teaching the Next Generations: A Comprehensive Guide for Teaching Christian Formation*, Terry Linhart, ed. (Grand Rapids, MI: Baker Academic, 2016), 101.

179 Smith, *Lost in Transition*, 241.

180 Packard, 47.

181 Christian Smith, *Souls in Transition: The Religious and Spiritual Lives of Emerging Adults* (New York, NY: Oxford University Press, 2009), 291.

182 Kinnaman, 115.

183 Kinnaman, 210.

184 Gary Newton, *Heart-Deep Teaching: Engaging Students for Transformed Lives* (Nashville, TN: B&H Academic, 2012), 125.

185 Elmore, *Marching off the Map*.

186 Ogden, 182.

187 Nathan C. Byrd "Narrative Discipleship: Guiding emerging adults to 'connect the dots' of life and faith," *Christian Education Journal*, Series 3, Vol. 8, No. 2 (2011), 246.

188 James K. Hampton, "Using Narrative to Invite Others into the Story of God," in *Teaching the Next Generations: A Comprehensive Guide for Teaching Christian Formation*, Terry Linhart, ed. (Grand Rapids, MI: Baker Academic, 2016), 249.

189 Tim LaFluer, *The Heart of a Disciplemaker: Building a Lasting Legacy Through Authentic Relationship* (Hendersonville, TN: Replicate Resources, 2017), 79.

190 Setran and Kiesling, 206.

191 Kinnaman, 217.

192 LaFleur, 86.

193 Smith, *Lost in Transition*, 241.

194 Ibid, 234.

195 Ibid, 235.

196 Ogden, 179.

Chapter 12:

197 Christian Standard Bible. Nashville: Holman Bible Publishers, 2017.

198 This is adapted from training and teaching Pat MacMillan, Building Powerful Ministry Teams, 2003., Atlanta. GA.

199 The section of *One Leader at a Time* is adapted from training and teaching as a Certified Facilitator for Ken Blanchards, Situational Leadership II, 2013., Escondido, CA.

200 James M. Kouzes and Barry Z. Posner, *The leadership challenge: how to make extraordinary things happen in organizations* (Hoboken, NJ: Leadership Challenge, A Wiley Brand, 2017), 258.

## Chapter 13:

201  US Census Bureau. The Nation's Older Population Is Still Growing, Census Bureau Reports. CB17-100, June 22. Accessed July 10, 2017. https://census.gov/ newsroom/pressreleases/2017/cb17-100.html.

202  US Census Bureau. Fueled by Aging Baby Boomers, Nation's Older Population to Nearly Double in the Next 20 Years, Census Bureau Reports. CB14-84, May 6, 2014. https://www.census.gov/newsroom/press-releases/2014/cb14-84.html.

203  Elizabeth J. Bergman, Mary Ann Erickson, and Jocelyn N. Simons, "Attracting and Training Tomorrow's Gerontologists," *Educational Gerontology* 40, no. 3 (2014): 182.

204  James M. Houston, and Michael Parker. *A Vision for the Aging Church: Renewing Ministry for and by Seniors* (Downers Grove, IL: InterVarsity Press, 2011), 42.

205  Robert L. Barker. *The Social Work Dictionary,* 6th ed. (Washington, DC: NASW Press, 2013), 12.

206  For information on generational ministry see: Amy Hanson. *Baby Boomers and Beyond: Tapping the Ministry Talents and Passions of Adults over 50.* (San Franciso, CA: Jossey-Bass, 2010) and Elisabeth A. Nesbit Sbanotto, and Craig L. Blomberg. *Effective Generational Ministry: Biblical and Practical Insights for Transforming Church Communities.* (Grand Rapids, MI: Baker Academic, 2016).

207  Carla M. Perissinotto, Irena Stijacic Cenzer, and Kenneth E. Covinsky. "Loneliness in Older Persons: A Predictor of Functional Decline and Death," *Archives of Internal Medicine* 172, no 14 (July 23, 2012): 1081, accessed July 10, 2017, http://dx.doi.org/10.1001/ achinternmed.2012.1993.

208  National Center for Health Statistics. *Health, United States, 2016: With Chartbook on Long-term Trends in Health* (Hyattsville, MD, 2017).

## Chapter 14:

209  Robert Coleman, *The Master Plan of Evangelism* (Grand Rapids: Spire Publishing 2010), 21.

210  Patrick Morley, *No Man Left Behind: How to Build and Sustain a Thriving, Disciple-Making Ministry for Every Man in Your Church* (Chicago: Moody Publishers, 2006), 41.

211  Dr. Jay Strack, conversation with author, Washington DC., 25, July 2013.

## Chapter 15:

212  Sue Edwards and Barbara Neumann, *Organic Mentoring: A Mentor's Guide to Relationships with Next Generation Women,* (Grand Rapids, MI: Kregel Ministry, 2014), 15.

213  Ibid, 27.

214  Chris Adams, ed., *Women Reaching Women, Meeting Needs Through Groups by Rhonda H. Kelley,* (Nashville, TN: LifeWay Press, 2015), 147.

215  Chris Adams, ed., *Women Reaching Women, Conferences and Retreats by Merci Dixon,* (Nashville, TN: LifeWay Press, 2015), 147

216  *Organic Mentoring,* 15.

CPSIA information can be obtained
at www.ICGtesting.com
Printed in the USA
LVHW100534180123
737338LV00001B/41

9 781973 619635